SOCRATES

In the Golden Age of Greece, Socrates lived much of his life, free to go among men seeking the truth. From the Oracle of Delphi, Socrates took the divine command to test and question men. He believed it was his mission to expose folly and false wisdom.

Unlike many philosophers of his day, his concern was with the personal conduct of life, the nature of law and morality, the relation of man to his country. Unlike the Sophists, Socrates never gave lectures, nor took payment, nor wrote down his philosophy. His was a truth found through self-examination; his was a method of constant questioning.

Robert Silverberg not only writes a factual account of Socrates, the philosopher, the soldier, the Athenian, but also captures the tenor of ancient Greece and one of her most venerable men.

SOCRATES

By

ROBERT SILVERBERG

G. P. Putnam's Sons

New York

Contents

SOCRATES

1

❖ ❖ ❖

Enter Socrates—Talking

ONE DAY in the year we call 399 B.C., two men met by chance in the law court of Athens. One was young and foolish, the other old and wise. They both had business to attend to in the court.

The young man's name was Euthyphro. He would be completely forgotten today but for the conversation he had with the older man. Although Euthyphro was young, he fancied himself as being quite learned. He had devoted his life to the service of the gods, and above all tried to be a just and pious man. He took himself rather seriously, it seems. We can imagine that when he walked through the crowded streets of Athens, he kept aloof from other men, with his nose in the air. For Euthyphro thought that he was more virtuous than other men, and therefore better than they were.

Next to him, the other man, whose name was Socrates,

looked clownish and grotesque. Socrates was seventy years old, and had none of young Euthyphro's stiff dignity. Instead, he looked as coarse and as earthy as a peasant. He was a short man, very stocky, with wide shoulders and a deep chest. Although he was well along in years, Socrates gave an impression of great physical strength. All he wore was a thin robe, tattered and patched. His feet were bare, and from the calloused look of them it was obvious that he hadn't worn shoes or sandals very often.

And Socrates was an ugly man. His ugliness was practically a joke in Athens. Many years before, a handsome, popular young Athenian named Alcibiades, who had been a close friend of Socrates, had compared him to the little figures of Silenus that were sold in many shops. Since Silenus, in the Greek myths, was always shown as a fat, bald-headed, pug-nosed old man half drunk on wine, it was not much of a compliment.

Socrates was not as drunken as Silenus—indeed, nobody in Athens had ever seen Socrates get drunk at all, though he was fond of wine. But in other ways he was very much a Silenus. He was bald, with bulging eyes and a flat nose and wide, flaring nostrils. His mouth was wide, too, with thick, coarse lips. He had a short neck, so that his big head seemed to sprout right from his husky shoulders. Altogether, not a very elegant sight!

Everybody in Athens knew Socrates well. He was always to be found somewhere in the city, perhaps in the market place, perhaps in the gymnasium, perhaps in some rich man's home—talking. Always talking. Always asking questions. Very disturbing questions they were, too. Socrates had a gift for asking questions that could leave a man dizzy.

Socrates had made many enemies for himself, thanks to

his endless questions. When someone fell into conversation with him, that person often went away angry and embarrassed, because Socrates had shown him to be a fool. Even the friends of Socrates spoke with amusement about the perils of talking to Socrates. As one of them, Nicias, had put it:

"Anyone who enters into conversation with Socrates is liable to be drawn into an argument; and whatever subject he may start, he will be continually carried round and round by him, until at last he finds that he has to give an account both of his present and past life. And when he is once entangled, Socrates will not let him go until he has completely and thoroughly sifted him."

Some people came away wiser for having been entangled and sifted by Socrates. Others simply stalked away, grumbling in wrath. Enough Athenians had been offended by Socrates so that, on this particular day, he had to come to court to answer serious charges. He was accused of being a subversive—of having gone around Athens saying and teaching things that were dangerous and unpatriotic.

But though he was about to go on trial, Socrates did not seem disturbed as he arrived at the law court. He was as relaxed and as inquisitive as ever. There was plenty of time, before the trial, to indulge in his favorite hobby—asking questions.

And so young Euthyphro was added to the list of Socrates' victims. He found himself carried round and round by the ugly old man's questions, found himself "entangled" and "sifted." It happens that we have some idea of what Euthyphro and Socrates spoke of that day, because Socrates later repeated the gist of the conversation to a young disciple of his named Plato, and Plato wrote it down. So, by way of getting to see what sort of a man

Socrates was and how he went about his search for truth, let us look at Plato's account of his talk with Euthyphro.

Euthyphro was surprised to see Socrates in the law court at all. "What in the world are you doing here?" he asked. "You surely haven't come to place a suit before the judges, as I have."

Socrates smiled ironically. "The Athenians, Euthyphro, call it an indictment, not a suit."

"What? Do you mean that someone is prosecuting you? Who is he?"

"I scarcely know him myself," Socrates replied. "He is some young man named Meletus—a hook-nosed man with lanky hair and rather a scanty beard."

"I don't know him, Socrates. But tell me, what is he prosecuting you for?"

The old man's eyes twinkled with merriment. "He says I am corrupting the youth of Athens. And he says I have invented new gods and do not believe in the old ones."

Euthyphro thought it was a ridiculous charge, and said so. Nothing will come of the indictment, he told Socrates. "Very likely you will be successful in your trial, and I think I shall be in mine."

"And what is this suit of yours, Euthyphro?" Socrates asked. "Are you suing, or being sued?"

"I am suing," he answered. Euthyphro explained that the man he had brought action against, on a charge of murder, was his own father!

Socrates seemed astounded at that. Accusing your own father of murder? "Only a very wise man would dare to do something like that," Socrates said. "Only one who is very sure that his course is just."

"That is quite true, Socrates," Euthyphro replied smugly.

So Euthyphro was claiming to be wise! That was just the sort of thing Socrates loved to attack. And he lost no time going to work on the pious and learned Euthyphro.

"Was the man your father killed a relative of yours?" Socrates asked. "But, of course, he was. You would never have prosecuted your father for the murder of a stranger!"

"You amuse me, Socrates. What difference does it make whether the murdered man was a relative or a stranger? Murder must be punished!" And, Euthyphro explained, the dead man was no relative at all, but simply a slave, a laborer who worked on the farm of Euthyphro's father. The laborer had gotten drunk and killed another slave. Euthyphro's father had bound the man hand and foot, and had left him in a ditch while a messenger went to Athens to get advice on what to do with him. The messenger had been slow in returning, and Euthyphro's father had forgotten all about the slave in the ditch. Soon the man was dead of hunger and cold.

"My father and my family are indignant with me because I am prosecuting my father for the murder of this murderer," Euthyphro said. "They argue that he didn't kill the man at all, and they say that, even if he had killed him over and over again, the man himself was a murderer. They say I ought not to concern myself about such a person because it is impious for a son to prosecute a father for murder." And Euthyphro drew himself up haughtily, relishing his own wisdom and virtue. "So little, Socrates, do they know the divine law of piety and impiety!"

"Oh?" Socrates said, skeptically cocking an eyebrow. "And you think you understand such things so well that you can bring your father to justice without fear that you yourself may be doing an impious deed?"

Euthyphro admitted modestly that he did have superior

knowledge of piety and impiety. Whereupon Socrates said, "Then, my excellent Euthyphro, I cannot do better than become your pupil. For I am soon to go on trial for my impiety. Teach me what is pious and what is impious, so I can best defend myself against my accusers."

Socrates was having some fun with Euthyphro. It was absurd to think that this wise old man needed to make himself a pupil of the self-important youngster. But Euthyphro failed to see that he was being teased. He promptly agreed to give Socrates the benefit of his wisdom.

"Tell me, then," Socrates asked, "what is piety and what is impiety?"

Euthyphro answered promptly, "Piety means prosecuting the wrongdoer who has committed murder or sacrilege, or any other such crime, as I am doing now, whether he is your father or your mother or whoever he is. And I say that impiety means not prosecuting him."

He gave several examples from the Greek myths—such as Zeus, chief of the gods, who overthrew his own father, Cronos, when Cronos committed evil. If Euthyphro had done anything wrong by bringing his father to justice, well, so then had Zeus.

"And do you believe the stories people tell about the gods?" Socrates asked.

"Certainly I do," Euthyphro said. He admitted that he believed there was war among the gods, and bitter hatred, and battles, such as the poets and painters had depicted.

Now Socrates sprung the trap. "We are trying to find out which actions are pious and which are impious. Would you say that what is pleasing to the gods is pious, and what is not pleasing to them is impious?"

"Certainly."

"But have we not also said, Euthyphro, that there are

quarrels and disagreements and hatreds among the gods?"

"We have."

"And do the gods quarrel over matters of right and
wrong, of the honorable and dishonorable, of the good and
the bad?"

"Yes, Socrates, they do."

"Then, my good Euthyphro, you say that some of the
gods think one thing right, and others, another; and that
what some of them hold to be honorable or good, others
hold to be dishonorable or evil. For there would not have
been quarrels among them if they had not disagreed on
these points, would there?"

"You are right," admitted the baffled Euthyphro.

"Then the same thing is hated by the gods and loved by
them," Socrates said. "And the same thing will be displeas-
ing and pleasing to them."

"Apparently."

"Then, according to your account, the same thing will
be both pious and impious."

Euthyphro was aghast. Socrates had led him, by skillful
questioning, to a conclusion that was pure nonsense!

Nor was the old man finished. The gods, he said, all
agreed that if one man kills another wrongfully, he must
be punished. No one disagreed with that. The disagreement was over deciding what was right and what was
wrong. "And what proof have you, Euthyphro, that all the
gods think it is wrong when a laborer who has been im-
prisoned for murder by the master of the man whom he
has murdered, and who dies from his imprisonment before
the master has had time to learn what he should do, dies
wrongfully? How do you know that it is right for a son to
indict his father and to prosecute him for the murder of
such a man?"

Euthyphro was squirming. He had come to court absolutely convinced he was doing the right thing. In a few minutes of talk, Socrates had completely shaken his confidence.

The old man suggested a new definition. "Shall we say that whatever *all* the gods hate is impious, and whatever they all love is pious; while whatever some of them love, and others hate, is either both or neither? Do you wish us now to define piety and impiety this way?"

"Why not, Socrates? Piety is what all the gods love, I should say, and impiety is what they all hate."

"And shall we examine this definition, Euthyphro, and see if it is a good one?"

"Yes," Euthyphro said. "But for my part I think that the definition is right this time."

"We shall know that better in a little while, my good friend," said Socrates, smiling. And he launched into a new line of questions that left Euthyphro more confused than ever. Socrates now wanted Euthyphro to tell him the nature of piety. Euthyphro was simply saying that piety was "what all the gods love"—but that was only an aspect of piety, not its definition. When we say of water, "It is what quenches the thirst," we are mentioning a fact *about* water, but we are not saying much about what water really is. And so it was with Euthyphro and piety.

In short order, Socrates was able to show Euthyphro that his new definition would not do, either. Euthyphro, looking troubled and confused, said, "No matter what statement we put forward, it always somehow moves round in a circle, and will not stay where we put it."

Socrates, like all great teachers, was very patient when helping someone grope toward the truth. Now he offered, through more questions, to help Euthyphro explain what piety was. "Don't give in yet," Socrates said. "Tell me, do you not think that all piety must be just?"

"I do."

"Well, then, is all justice pious, too? Or, while all piety is just, is only a part of justice pious, and the rest of it something else?"

Euthyphro blinked in bewilderment. "I do not follow you, Socrates."

Socrates spelled it out. The idea of number, he said, included both the odd and even. But where you had number, you did not always have the odd. So, too, justice included piety and other things too, did it not? If so, what part of justice was piety?

"I should say," Euthyphro replied, "that righteousness and piety are that part of justice which has to do with the attention which is due to the gods; and that what has to do with the attention due to men is the remaining part of justice."

"Then piety is the care of the gods? I suppose you do not mean that the care which we show to the gods is like the care we show to other things," Socrates said. "We say, for instance, do we not, that not everyone knows how to take care of horses, but only the trainer of horses?"

"Certainly."

"And not everyone understands the care of cattle, but only the herdsman?"

"True."

"And you say that piety and righteousness mean the care of the gods, Euthyphro?"

"I do."

"Well, then, has not all care the same object? Horses and cattle are benefited and improved when they receive skilled care. Is it not so?"

"Of course."

"Then is piety, which is the care we bestow on the gods, intended to benefit the gods, or to improve them?" Socrates asked. "Should you allow that you make any of the gods better when you do a pious action?"

"No, indeed. Certainly not."

"Then what sort of attention to the gods will piety be?"

"The attention, Socrates, of slaves to their masters," said Euthyphro.

"I understand. Then it is a kind of service to the gods?"

"Certainly."

"But every service has a purpose. A doctor serves to produce health. A shipwright serves to build ships. What result does piety, the art which serves the gods, produce?"

"The results are many and noble," Euthyphro said.

"Yes, but what are they?" Socrates prodded.

"It is not so easy to speak accurately in these matters," muttered Euthyphro. "But broadly, I say this: if any man knows that his words and deeds in prayer and sacrifice are acceptable to the gods, that is what is pious. It preserves the commonwealth. The opposite of what is acceptable to the gods brings ruin and destruction on all things."

"Then piety is a science of prayer and sacrifice? Is that what you mean?"

"I do."

"To sacrifice is to give to the gods, and to pray is to ask of them, is it not?"

"It is, Socrates."

"Then you say that piety is the science of asking of the gods and giving to them?"

"You understand my meaning exactly, Socrates."

"Then to ask rightly will be to ask of them what we need from them, will it not?"

"Naturally," Euthyphro said. He was smiling again, for now he felt he was certainly on the right track in this debate with the troublesome Socrates.

"And to give rightly will be to give back to them what they stand in need of from us?"

"True, Socrates."

"But what *are* these gifts, Euthyphro, that we give the gods?"

"What do you think they are but honor and homage?"

"Then piety is acceptable to the gods," Socrates said. "Is it not then loved by them?"

"I think that nothing is more loved by them."

"Then I see that piety means that which is loved by the gods."

Euthyphro frowned again, for the argument was coming around in a circle again. "Most certainly," he said.

But only a short while before, the discussion had reached the point that piety could not be defined simply as "what the gods love." And now Euthyphro had said once again that piety was what is pleasing to the gods.

"If we were right before," Socrates said, "then we are wrong now."

"So it seems," Euthyphro said glumly.

"Then we must begin again and inquire what is piety. I do not mean to give in until I have found out. Give your whole mind to the question, Euthyphro, and this time tell me the truth. For if anyone knows it, it is you. It cannot be that you would ever have undertaken to prosecute your aged father for the murder of a laboring man unless you had known exactly what is piety and impiety. You would have feared to risk the anger of the gods, in case you should be doing wrong, and you would have been afraid of what men would say. So tell me, my good Euthyphro, what is piety and what is not, and do not conceal from me what you hold it to be."

Euthyphro, however, had had quite enough of this discussion. Socrates had quietly and efficiently shaken up every idea in Euthyphro's head, and the unhappy young man wanted nothing more now than to escape. "Another time, then, Socrates," he stammered. "I am in a hurry now, and it is time for me to be off."

Euthyphro broke free of Socrates and hurried into the law court. The conversation was over. Once again, Socrates had worked his wiles.

Had he taught Euthyphro anything? Had he given the young man one bit of information? Or had he simply asked a lot of meddlesome questions?

Socrates had done only one thing for Euthyphro. He had planted the seed of doubt in the young man's mind. Euthyphro had come to court certain that he knew all about piety and impiety. Socrates had shown him that he did not really know anything at all. He had forced Euthyphro to re-examine all his ideas. He had made Euthyphro *think*.

Thinking often gives people headaches, especially when they are not in the habit of thinking for themselves. Socrates had given all of Athens a great headache of that sort. Talking, always talking, he had left the whole city troubled about the basic ideas of existence. It did not make him a popular man.

And so Socrates slowly walked into the law court himself, to stand trial on charges of stirring up trouble in Athens. He faced a penalty of death. And there were many in Athens, that day, who hoped the old troublemaker would be silenced at last.

2

❖ ❖ ❖

A Golden Age

Socrates was an unusual man, and he lived in an unusual city at an unusual time. The best way we can begin to understand him is to know something of the city that produced him.

He was a man of Greece. He thought of himself, though, not as a Greek but as an Athenian. Athens, like the other cities of Greece, was a city-state, independent and self-governing. Though Greece is a fairly small place, there were hundreds of these city-states. Some were wealthy and proud; others were poor, huddling in the protective shadows of their neighbors. When Socrates was born, about 470 B.C., Athens was the greatest city-state of Hellas, which is what the Greeks called their motherland. Socrates grew up in the golden age of Athens.

It was a wonderful time to be alive. Athens hummed with vitality and energy. The electric crackle of new ideas could be heard everywhere. For 50 years, little Athens was the center of the world. Every important thinker, every important artist and sculptor and playwright dwelled in Athens. The city's intellectual life was rivaled only by its commercial wealth. It was indeed a golden age, and Socrates lived through it all, living on into the sad time of Athens' decline.

There have not been many such golden ages. Perhaps the England of Queen Elizabeth I was like that, with Shakespeare and Marlowe and Ben Jonson writing their great plays, and Walter Raleigh and Sir Francis Drake bringing England glory on the high seas. Perhaps Philadelphia in Ben Franklin's time had some of the quality of old Athens. Perhaps Florence in the Renaissance, the Florence of Leonardo da Vinci and Benvenuto Cellini, had something of old Athens about it. But few other cities can claim to be the equal of Athens in the days of Socrates.

The greatness of Athens had its beginnings about 600 B.C. Before that time, Greece was an unimportant land, struggling up out of barbarism. (Once, perhaps about 1200 B.C., the Greeks had been a mighty people, who had waged war against the rich city of Troy in Asia Minor. But that old Greek civilization had collapsed under the weight of invasion by savage tribesmen, and only the poems of Homer kept its memory alive.)

By 600 B.C., the savage invaders had become civilized themselves, and Greece was growing wealthy again. Olive groves and vineyards dotted the valleys between the rugged mountains of Hellas. A rising class of merchants, shipowners, and workingmen had developed and was demanding a voice in government. The Greek cities had been ruled by nobles, descendants of old warrior chieftains. But this aristocracy was challenged by the new class, and great changes resulted.

The Greek word that we translate as "city-state" was *polis*.* It is a hard word to translate accurately. It means much more than the actual city itself, the buildings and streets. It takes in the idea of statehood, of independence. And it refers also to that intangible, invisible sense of community, that feeling of something held in common with one's neighbors. A man had great loyalty to his polis. The polis survived, even if the city itself were burned and all its people uprooted. The story of Greece is the story of the polis—of that fierce loyalty to home and neighbors and laws.

Each polis of Greece developed in its own individual way. Originally, many of them were ruled by kings. The kings gave way to a small ruling clique of wealthy landowners. Such a form of government was known as *oligarchy*, the rule of the few. At first, oligarchy did not work well. The oligarchs were too grasping, too selfish. In polis after polis, the oligarchs were in turn overthrown, and in each polis one man seized power by force. This is the kind of government known as *tyranny*.

Not all the tyrants were cruel and sinister. The word "tyrant" did not then have the same shade of meaning it has today, and some of the Greek tyrants ruled wisely and well. They prepared the way for other forms of government. Some of the tyrants, having brought order to their cities, yielded to new oligarchies. But in Athens something quite different happened. The world's first democracy appeared.

Athens is in eastern Greece, on a triangular peninsula called Attica. It did not become an important city until

* The English word "politics" is derived from *polis*.

fairly late in ancient Greek history, when it absorbed several small neighboring city-states of Attica. During the
seventh century before Christ, Athens was troubled by
conflict between the aristocrats and the common people,
and civil war threatened many times.

In 621 B.C., the nobles of Athens called in a man named
Draco to establish a new code of law. Draco's laws were
severe, so much so that even today a harsh law is sometimes
called "Draconian." But he succeeded in establishing the
rule of law in Athens for the first time. No longer could a
man who felt he was wronged take justice into his own
hands, by starting a private feud. Draco put Athens on the
road toward justice.

His laws were so harsh, though, that they were often
difficult to enforce. And many Athenians felt that the code
of Draco favored the rich too much. New trouble erupted;
by 594, another lawgiver had to be invited to help Athens
govern itself. His name was Solon. Solon's laws were
milder than Draco's, and gave important new powers to
the ordinary people of Athens.

In Draco's time, Athens had been ruled by three different groups. First, there was the Assembly, made up of all
citizens who owned property. The Assembly could meet to
discuss the way Athens was being governed, but it had
little real power. Next, there were the nine *archons,* or
executive officers, who were elected by the Assembly to
serve one-year terms. Finally, there was the Council of the
Areopagus, so named because it met on the hill of Ares,
the war god. The Council of the Areopagus was made up
of former archons. It held the real power in Athens.

Only a wealthy aristocrat could become an archon, and
only the most important archons ever came to have much
influence in the Areopagus. Solon changed that. No longer

did one have to be of noble birth to be an archon. Commoners also might hold that position provided they owned property. For the first time, the new class of wealthy but common-born merchants had a voice in the government of Athens.

Solon also expanded the Assembly. Now all citizens, even those without property, would belong to the Assembly. That made it somewhat unwieldy, so Solon accordingly provided for a Council of Four Hundred, elected by the Assembly, which would meet to decide on the issues the Assembly was to discuss. And Solon set up courts of justice. The judges in these courts were ordinary citizens, chosen by lot from among the members of the Assembly.

By 560 B.C., when Solon retired, nearly every Athenian had some say in the way his city was run. Of course, Athens was quite a small city, by our standards. In the time of Socrates, Athens had only about 350,000 people. Of these, 150,000 were slaves, and did not count as citizens. Some 30,000 more were *metics*, citizens of other lands who lived in Athens, doing business there but not enjoying the right to vote. The remaining 170,000 Athenians were citizens, but many of these were women and children, who were not allowed to vote either. The adult male population— the voters—numbered only about 40,000. In their hands rested the government of Athens.

Solon's system was a bit ahead of its time. Athens was not quite ready for democracy—the rule of *demos,* the people. An aristocrat named Pisistratus seized power when Solon stepped down. However, the new tyrant was wise enough to preserve Solon's reforms. He allowed the people of Athens to share in the making of decisions, and he broke up the estates of some nobles to give land to the poor.

Pisistratus, and his two sons who followed him, prepared the way for the real Athenian democracy that was to come.

Pisistratus was also a patron of the arts. He built a temple to Athens' special goddess, the wise Athena, and another to great Zeus. To decorate these temples, he brought sculptors and artists from the Greek colonies of Ionia, on the coast of Asia Minor. The Ionians taught the Athenians much about sculpture and architecture. The old, wooden buildings of Athens began to give way to magnificent new structures of gleaming marble.

Poets came to Athens, too. Anacreon, whose lively verses were recited everywhere in Greece, took up residence there. The lyric poet Simonides came to live at the court of Pisistratus. The art of literature flowered. Then Athens invented an art form of her own—the theater.

For many years, Athenians had celebrated the festival of Dionysus, the god of wine, with songs and dances. First a chorus had appeared at the festivals to sing of the adventures of the tipsy god. Then, one year, the leader of the chorus stepped forward to sing solo verses, with the chorus answering him. Before long, instead of simply singing *about* Dionysus, the leader of the chorus began to impersonate him, to play the part of the god. Then a second actor became part of the performance. There would be dialogues on stage. Poets began to invent plots and characters. Now not only Dionysus stories were told, but stories out of the other Greek myths, and out of Homer. Some plays were serious and somber, the tragedies; others, the comedies, were wildly funny, poking fun at anything and anybody.

In the time of Pisistratus, the new art form got official recognition. The tyrant set up a competition, in 534, with prizes for the best plays each year. All of Athens would gather in the open-air Theater of Dionysus to watch the plays, and the merits of each playwright would be hotly debated. The theater was something uniquely Athenian.

After half a century, the family of Pisistratus lost its grip on Athens. Hipparchus, one son of Pisistratus, was assassinated in 514, and a few years later his brother Hippias was driven into exile by a conspiracy of noblemen. The new ruler, an aristocrat named Clisthenes, proved to be as just as the tyrants he had replaced. He completed the job of creating the Athenian democracy.

Clisthenes broke the strength of the old Athenian tribes, the aristocratic families who had been powerful for so long. He divided Attica into 100 districts known as *demes,* which cut across the old tribal lines. He divided the demes into ten new "tribes" of ten demes each, so arranging it that each of these new tribes included representatives of every Attican group—the mountain-dwellers, the city people, the coastal inhabitants.

He also admitted many of the foreign-born metics to citizenship. And he ruled that the son of an Athenian citizen was automatically a citizen himself, even if his mother was a foreigner. Former slaves, too, were admitted to citizenship. All this did much to weaken the power of the old aristocrats.

In the Athens of Clisthenes, the legislative, or law-*making* power, rested with the Assembly. It met at least ten times every year, always in the open air, to vote on laws and elect the chief officials of the city. Since the Assembly now had many thousands of members, it was guided by a Council of Five Hundred, modeled after the Council of Four Hundred of Solon.

The Council of Five Hundred was chosen each year by the citizens of each deme. It was divided into ten committees of 50 citizens, and each committee guided the government for a tenth of the year. No man could belong to the Council for more than two years, which meant that nearly every citizen of Athens had a chance to serve on it during his lifetime.

A different man presided over the Council every day, and no one could hold that office twice. The "chairman" of the Council thus held the highest office in Athens—but only for 24 hours!

There was no civil service in Athens, no bureaucracy. The men who made up the government were ordinary citizens who took time off from their work to serve on the Council, just as today the juries of our courts are made up of men and women picked by lot from the rolls of citizens. The Athenian executive power, the law-*enforcing* power, was in the hands of this ever-changing Council of Five Hundred.

The other branch of the government, the judicial, was run the same way. Each year the demes elected 6,000 men to serve in the courts. An important trial might require the services of 100 or more men drawn from this pool. The citizens were both judge and jury; they reached the verdicts, and decided on the sentences.

Of course, even this system did not lead to pure democracy. There was always one Athenian more influential than all the others, one man whose voice was heard above the rest. Draco, Solon, Pisistratus, Hippias, Hipparchus and Clisthenes had all played such a role in Athens. After Clisthenes, the central figure of Athens was usually one of the leading generals or admirals—for, by 500 B.C., the young democracy of Athens was faced by the threat of war.

The enemy was Persia. This sprawling Asiatic state had conquered the older empires of Assyria and Babylonia, and under Cyrus the Great, who ruled from 559 to 530, had become the supreme power of the world. The son of Cyrus had added old Egypt to the Persian domain. Asia Minor, too, fell to the Persians, and the Greek cities of Ionia became Persian property.

The Ionians chafed under Persian rule. They rebelled against Persia's King Darius, and in 498 B.C., 25 Greek ships, 20 of them sent from Athens, made so bold as to cross the sea and help the Ionians invade Persian territory.

Like an elephant stung by a mosquito, mighty Persia turned to slap down the annoying Greeks. In 492, Darius sent a fleet to invade Greece, but it was shattered in a storm. Two years later, he tried again. Persian armies marched across Greek soil. On September 21, 490, the men of Athens, under a general named Miltiades, met the Persians in grim confrontation. And—wonder of wonders!— the upstart Greeks won the battle, sending the Persians fleeing helter-skelter!

The shock of that defeat reverberated through the world. Persia had tasted defeat for the first time since her rise to greatness. Ten years later, Darius' successor, Xerxes, tried to avenge the defeat at Marathon, only to meet even more stunning defeat at the battle of Salamis. The following spring, the Persians succeeded in invading Athens and burning the city, but it was their only triumph. The Athenians inflicted two more setbacks on the Persian navy in August, 479, and after that the independence of Athens was assured.

Now the golden age of Athens began. Athens towered above the city-states of Hellas. She was the richest and the strongest, and her valor had been proved in battle. Had not Xerxes crept away to lick his wounds sullenly in Persia? Had not Athenians held off the Persian conqueror when all seemed darkest?

The cities of Greece, in 476, formed a league to defend their homeland against further Persian menace. It was not a federation or a union. Each polis remained independent and sovereign. But each agreed to contribute money or ships, which would be turned over to Athens and used in the common defense. Because the league's headquarters were on the sacred isle of Delos, supposedly the birthplace of Apollo, it was known as the League of Delos. But it might just as well have been called the Athenian League.

Athens glittered now. Splendid marble temples shimmered in the brilliant sunlight. Ships thronged the Piraeus, Athens' port. Merchants of many lands did business in the Athenian marketplace. At the Theater of Dionysus, Athenians applauded the plays of the great Aeschylus. In one of his plays, Aeschylus turned away from mythological themes to tell the story of the downfall of the Persians, and all Athens acclaimed the playwright who had served heroically at Marathon.

The leadership of Athens passed through the hands of the men who had waged the successful war against Persia. Gradually, the old leaders lost favor, and new men arose. The most important was Cimon, son of Miltiades, the victorious general of Marathon. The Assembly of Athens elected Cimon to be one of the city's ten generals, and he led the ships of the Delian League in a series of new victories over the Persians. The League itself grew until it included more than 200 cities, most of them on the islands of the Aegean or along the seacoasts of Greece. The League rapidly turned into an Athenian Empire. By 454, the headquarters of the League was shifted from Delos to Athens, by way of acknowledging Athens' pre-eminence.

Athenian coins, stamped with the owl of Athens, were common currency throughout the cities of the League.

Cimon died about 450 B.C. His place as Athens' leader had already been taken by his kinsman by marriage, Pericles. Pericles had come to power in 461, when Cimon's popularity waned. The golden age of Athens is often called simply the Age of Pericles, for during his time Athens reached the peak of her greatness.

In the Age of Pericles, Athens was at peace with Persia, and her enemies in Greece itself were not yet strong enough to challenge her. Athens grew mightier and wealthier with each passing year.

It was Pericles who transformed the Delian League openly into an Athenian Empire. Now it became impossible for any member of the League to withdraw. Those cities that tried to secede were compelled by force to continue making their contributions to the League treasury. Herself a democracy, Athens had come to be the tyrant of Greece. For the sake of protecting Greece against outside enemies, Athens found it necessary to rob her fellow city-states of their full freedom.

But Athens did not oppress her neighbors. Her demands were light. And all Greece shared in the new prosperity the League had created. Ships of the League kept pirates off the seas, and guarded against Persian attack. Merchant vessels now moved safely from city to city. Athens' system of law was admired and copied in many parts of Greece. The rich cultural life of Athens attracted outstanding men from all over.

This was the time when a second great playright, Sophocles, was giving Athenians his *King Oedipus, Antigone,* and *Electra.* The marble splendor of the Parthenon was rising on the hill known as the Acropolis, adorned by statues carved by the famed sculptor, Phidias. Herodotus, a Greek from Asia Minor, had come to Athens and was reading Athenians his book on the Persian Wars—the first book of history ever written.

There were philosophers in Athens, too. Athens was a kind of clearinghouse for ideas, and any man who thought he had something important to say came to Athens to say it. Athens was not the birthplace of Greek philosophy. That was in Asia Minor, among the Ionian Greeks. About 600 B.C., men of the Ionian cities began to ponder the mysteries of the world about them, to ask questions and seek answers. What was the world made of? Why were living things different from dead things? What was the soul? What was the mind? What was the difference between air and water? The Ionians were full of such questions.

By the time of Pericles, many of these questioners had come to Athens. Half a dozen conflicting schools of philosophy had developed, because different wise men had different answers to the great questions. For a fee, the wise men would impart their wisdom to seekers after knowledge. And the Athenians, eager to know everything, hurried from teacher to teacher, and then engaged in noisy disputes about the nature of the universe. Athens boiled with ideas.

One of the philosophers of the time of Pericles was that ugly, snub-nosed little man, Socrates. Unlike the others, he accepted no fees and taught no lessons. He had no "system" to give the world. He told everyone he was searching for the truth himself—while the other philosophers, who offered truth for sale, thought they had already found it.

He must have cut an odd figure in that golden age. There were many handsome men in Athens, with Pericles

one of the most handsome of all. Athenians spent much of
their time outdoors, swimming and engaging in games,
and they grew up straight and tall and healthy. It was a
city of lean, tanned, graceful men. And among them
walked Socrates, short and burly, looking for all the world
like one of those comic clay figures of Silenus, come to
life.

Phidias created noble statues. Pericles built a great empire. Aeschylus and Sophocles wrote plays that have lasted
through the centuries. Herodotus invented history.

And Socrates? He wrote nothing, left nothing after him
but some anecdotes of his life and thought. In an era of
creative genius, Socrates created nothing.

All he did was ask questions—day and night, year after
year. He was the man who *asked*.

3

❖ ❖ ❖

The Stonemason's Son

About the year 470 B.C., a child was born to Sophroniscus, a stonemason or sculptor of Athens, and his wife,
Phaenarete, who was a midwife by trade. The baby boy,
who probably was not very pretty, was named Socrates.

It was a good time to be born. Persia, that paper tiger,
had been thumped resoundingly in battle after battle, and
Athenians no longer had to fear that the soldiers of Xerxes
would swarm into their city. Athens had recovered from its
burning at the hands of the Persians in 479, the new city
rising proudly on the ruins of the old. The League of
Delos was six years old, and the brave fleet of the League
kept the sea clear of enemies.

The leading figure of Athens was Cimon, son of Miltiades. Then, too, there was Pericles, almost 30 years old,
already respected and popular—obviously the man to
watch in Athenian politics.

Socrates' parents were common people, but not poor. Sophroniscus had plenty of work to do, for his craftsmanship in stone was much admired, and Athens was a growing city with a great demand for sculptors. Phaenarete, too, was a busy woman. She was such a skillful midwife that many wellborn Athenians made use of her services to help bring their babies into the world.

We know hardly anything at all about the early years of Socrates. Sophroniscus quite naturally expected the boy to follow the same trade as his father, and so Socrates was given training as a stonemason. But he also received a general education in what we might call the liberal arts. He became familiar with the epics of Homer and the poetry of Hesiod, who long ago had chronicled the doings of the gods. He was acquainted with the plays of Aeschylus and Sophocles, of course. He knew something about Ionian science, about astronomy and geometry and arithmetic.

Mostly, though, Socrates was interested in questions of right and wrong. While most of the Greek philosophers were arguing over the cause of rain, or the reason for the falling of leaves in autumn, or the size of the moon, Socrates was pondering more basic issues. He wanted to know, for example, what was a man's proper duty to his polis. He wanted to know what actions were just and what were unjust. He wanted to know how a man could make himself more virtuous. "How can a man best care for his soul?" Socrates wanted to know. "How can he learn how to do what is right?"

These were odd questions for a young man to be asking. The philosophers who were teaching in Athens did not know what to answer. They were more concerned with scientific topics, with an understanding of the physical world.

The philosophers had many different theories. One early thinker, Thales of Miletus, had taught that everything in the universe was made up of different forms of water. His fellow citizen, Anaximenes, disagreed. The basic substance, he said, was air. Another man said that fire was the real basis of everything; still another, earth. A fifth school of philosophy went on to say that all matter was made up of mixtures of these four "elements"—earth, air, fire, water.

One of the best known of these teachers was Anaxagoras, an Ionian Greek born around 500 B.C. Like many brilliant Ionians of his day, Anaxagoras found his way to Athens, where he became the teacher and companion of Pericles himself. From 456 on, his teachings were widely followed in Athens, and Socrates, who was fourteen when Anaxagoras arrived, was deeply interested in what the great man had to say.

Anaxagoras brushed aside the theories of earth, air, fire and water. None of them was the basic thing of the universe, he said. What was at the bottom of all things was *nous*—mind, intellect, order. At first, said Anaxagoras, there had only been chaos in the universe. But then the force he called nous had transformed chaos into order, bringing into being the world and all things.

These ideas, vague though they sound to us, had a great appeal for young Socrates. He had already come to believe that there had to be some orderly, sensible plan behind the workings of the universe. And now Anaxagoras seemed to be saying that it was just so, that an intelligent organizer had shaped the universe according to a rational scheme. So for a while Socrates was a disciple of Anaxagoras, and of his leading pupil, Archelaus.

But then Anaxagoras began to use his theory of mind as

a foundation for all sorts of wild speculations about the creation of things. Socrates lost interest. He was concerned with moral and ethical problems, with questions of right and wrong, of mind and intellect. He did not care about the way the stars were made. "I have no head for natural science," he said with some amusement, and left Anaxagoras to go his own way.

So far as we know, Socrates worked at the sculptor's trade during his youth. There are stories of the work he did and, as late as 150 A.D., tourists who visited Athens were shown statues that were supposedly carved by Socrates. But those statues may be no more genuine than the claims of hundreds of inns in the United States that say "George Washington slept here." Everyone likes to be associated with a famous man.

Certainly Socrates gave up his trade early in life. Once he reached manhood, he did no money-earning work at all. He devoted himself full time to philosophy—to asking questions, and to trying to find the truth about man and his nature.

If he did no work, how did he support himself? Not very luxuriously, it seems. Socrates had simple tastes. A single tattered cloak was enough for him in all weather. He needed no fine robes or elegant shoes. He had no use for costly wines and elaborately prepared food. He could get along without a vast mansion in which to live.

Besides, Socrates seems to have inherited a little money from his father. At one time in his life he mentioned being worth about 500 drachmas, which a rich friend had invested for him. That was a fair amount of money, since the daily wage of a sculptor in Athens was one drachma. But it hardly made Socrates a rich man.

It made him a property-owner, though, which made

Socrates eligible to take part in all the activities of the Athenian government. Among other things, being a man of property gave him the obligation to serve in the Athenian army. Socrates was a soldier who saw action many times. And, we know, he was a very good soldier indeed.

He was born too late to fight against the Persians. By the time Socrates reached manhood, Athens had a new enemy, even more deadly than Persia: the city-state of Sparta, in the southern peninsula of Greece known as the Peloponnesus.

Sparta was a grim and bleak place, very much unlike Athens. Where Athens was merry and poetry-loving, Sparta was dour, chiefly interested in the arts of war. Where Athens was a seagoing, commercial power, Sparta was an inland state which depended on agriculture. And where Athens was a democracy in which every citizen had a voice in government, Sparta was an oligarchy ruled by a small band of warriors.

Like Athens, Sparta had her great lawgiver. His name was Lycurgus, and no one is quite sure when he lived, though it must have been before 700 B.C. The system Lycurgus established set up three classes in Sparta.

The Spartans proper, the citizens, were on top of the heap. They numbered about a tenth of the total population. The Spartans were the rulers and the soldiers. They did no other work. If a baby born into a Spartan family looked unhealthy or deformed, that baby was abandoned in the wilderness to die, for no sickly Spartans were wanted.

At the age of seven, a Spartan boy left his parents and began his military training. He went through a course of discipline that makes modern army training look like a restful vacation in comparison. Until the age of thirty, Spartan men continued to live in barracks, undergoing never-ending physical drill and often taking part in warfare.

The second class of people in Sparta were the *perioikoi,* the "dwellers-round-about." These were the people who had lived in Sparta before the invasion of the warrior tribes. They were farmers, laborers, miners, merchants—in short, they kept the economic life of Sparta going. They had no political rights, and they were forbidden to intermarry with the Spartans. On the other hand, they were spared from having to go to war, since the Spartans reserved that obligation and privilege for themselves. The life of the perioikoi was a comfortable one. They were not citizens, but they were not slaves, either. They were looked down upon by the Spartans, who sneered at them as mere shopkeepers and laborers. But probably the perioikoi did not mind that too much.

The third class in Sparta had a much less happy time of it. These were the *helots,* the slaves. They had no rights at all. They were the personal servants of the Spartans and the farm workers who produced the food that supported the warrior class. The helots lived a life of terror. They were not allowed to carry arms, except when they accompanied their masters to the battlefield. They could not assemble after dark. Any Spartan who fancied himself offended by a helot was perfectly free to strike him down. On a special day each year, every Spartan was given the right to murder one helot as he pleased, just for amusement. Naturally, there were bold helots who resented this system, and there was constant danger of a revolt by the slaves. Any helot who showed exceptional intelligence or independence of thought was likely to be put to death to keep him from starting trouble.

Sparta was governed by two kings who held office jointly. They did not rule unhindered, though. Much of the ruling power was in the hands of five *ephors*, or overseers, elected each year by vote of all the citizens. Also, there was an Assembly of Spartans. So there were elements of monarchy, oligarchy and democracy about the Spartan government. But the important point is that the whole government involved only a fraction of the people who lived in Sparta, with perhaps only one person out of 50 having anything at all to say about the way he was governed.

The rivalry between Athens and Sparta was an ancient one. The Spartans were the best soldiers of Greece, the Athenians the best sailors. It was the Athenians who took the lead in the war with Persia. Though the Spartans fought bravely on several occasions, they somehow failed to arrive in time for a number of key battles, leaving the Athenians to do all the work . . . and get all the credit.

The Spartans watched uncomfortably as Athens grew more powerful with each year. Sparta believed in oligarchy and in the independence of each polis. Athens, a democracy, believed in welding all the city-states together into one league with herself as its leader. With the League of Delos growing ever stronger, a collision between Athens and Sparta became inevitable.

All during the years of Socrates' boyhood, Athens and Sparta glowered menacingly at each other. It was very much what we would call a "cold war." The two rivals worked hard to build up a network of military alliances, such as NATO and the Warsaw Pact in the modern world. They accused each other bitterly of "aggression" and "imperialism." Now and then they came to blows, but never in a serious way. In 457, when Socrates was thirteen, one of these small skirmishes at Tanagra resulted in an Athenian defeat. Soon after, Athens and Sparta worked out a five-year truce.

It was an uneasy truce, marked by a great deal of "cold war" bickering. Neither side lost any opportunity to make itself stronger. Pericles, in particular, sensing that war with Sparta was bound to come, led Athens on to a great expansion of her empire. Up to now, Athens had been content to take only seacoast and island cities into the League of Delos. Now, she also tried to gain domination of the mainland.

Sparta, the leading mainland power, would not permit it. When the five-year truce expired, Sparta took prompt military steps to break up Athens' new mainland domain. War threatened, but at the last moment it was averted. In 446, Sparta and Athens signed another treaty, this time establishing a new truce to last 30 years. Athens agreed to give up her claim to a mainland empire. Sparta agreed not to meddle with the League of Delos or with any neutral cities. There was peace in Hellas—for a while.

Socrates was twenty-four when the Thirty Years' Peace was negotiated. He had been studying with Anaxagoras and Archelaus for about seven years, and probably he was already beginning to grow dissatisfied with Anaxagoras' teachings. Like many other young Athenians at this time, Socrates was taking time off for military training—for Pericles was building up the army.

Socrates became a *hoplite,* an infantryman who wore heavy bronze armor. Since the hoplites had to pay for their armor themselves, only men of property could hold such a rank. The hoplites fought in a close rank called a *phalanx,* and they could be formidable warriors, as the Persians had found out half a century before.

It was not long before Socrates had his first taste of actual combat. In 441, the city of Samos, an ally of Athens, quarreled with its neighbor Miletus, also an ally of Athens. Samos and Miletus, both Ionian cities, both members of the League of Delos, went to war with each other, and Miletus was badly beaten. Miletus asked Athens for help.

Athens, as head of the League, ordered Samos to observe a cease-fire and submit to arbitration of her dispute with Miletus. Samos refused. It was open defiance of Athens, and this Athens could not permit. The old fiction of the League of Delos as a group of states with equal powers and rights had long since given way to the reality of an Athenian Empire, and now Samos was trying to pull out of the Empire.

Pericles sailed for Samos at the head of a fleet of 40 ships. Among the soldiers aboard those ships was Socrates. Another who went was Archelaus, the disciple of Anaxagoras and the friend and teacher of Socrates.

Samos was quickly brought under Athenian control. The little group of oligarchs who had defied Pericles was driven out, and a democratic government set up. No sooner had Pericles left, though, than the oligarchs returned, leading an army of Persian mercenary soldiers. A second time, Samos revolted against Athens. A second time, Pericles lay siege to the city. But this time it was a long, hard struggle before Samos surrendered. It was the spring of 439 before Pericles returned to Athens in triumph, having brought rebellious Samos back into the fold.

We have no idea what part Socrates played in the war against Samos. We know he was there, and that, during a lull in the battle, he voyaged to the nearby Ionian city of

Chios, where he met the poet, Ion. Ion himself wrote an account of his visit with Socrates and Archelaus in 440. Another who visited Ion that same year was the great playwright of tragedies, Sophocles, who also served in the siege of Samos. Sophocles was fifteen years older than Socrates, and we do not know whether the snub-nosed philosopher and the author of *Oedipus* were friends. But certainly they knew each other. Not only had they served together in war, but they were fellow citizens of Athens, and in the Athens of Pericles, everyone knew everyone else.

The revolt of Samos taught Athens an important lesson. She had to keep close watch on the cities of her Delian League. Her only safety against the threat of Sparta lay in her alliances—but she had to make sure that her allies stayed loyal. So Athens took a tighter grip on the cities of the League. In 434, for example, she forbade the other cities of the League to coin their own money. From then on, Athenian money, which had always been the most widely circulated anyway, was the *only* money the League could use.

The right to coin money was one of a city-state's most prized rights. If Athens had taken that right away from her allies, what would she next take from them?

The tighter Athens' grip became, the more fearful her rivals grew. Something had to be done to stop her, they argued, before she swallowed up all Hellas. One city that was particularly uneasy was Corinth. Corinth, which lay midway between Athens and Sparta, was a seaport, and Athens' most powerful commercial rival. The Corinthians had no love for Sparta, but they feared Athens more. So they too began to build up a network of alliances. Pericles feared that, before long, Corinth and Sparta might join forces to smash mighty Athens.

There were new rumblings of war. The first came in the spring of 433, at Corcyra, an island city-state off the west coast of Greece. Corcyra had been founded long before by colonists from Corinth. Corcyra herself had later set up a colony of her own, Epidamnus. When a revolution broke out in Epidamnus, Corcyra refused to get involved, so the Epidamnians turned for help to Corcyra's mother-city, Corinth. A complicated political situation developed, in which Corinth and Corcyra soon found themselves at the brink of war.

Corcyra needed help, and turned to Athens. Always looking for new allies, the Athenians agreed to aid Corcyra. Attempts to negotiate peace failed; there was a naval clash between Athens and Corinth; the Corinthians were badly beaten. Corinth had more reason than ever to hate Athens, long an irksome rival and now an ally of Corinth's enemy Corcyra.

The Corinthians brooded over their defeat. But the Corcyra-Corinth-Athens affair had not involved Sparta at all. Corinth looked about for some way to draw Sparta into war with Athens, war that Corinth could join on the Spartan side.

And soon there was new trouble, this time far to the north, in the region known as Chalcidice. Corinth had another colony there, Potidaea. Potidaea had come under Athenian domination, and had to pay a heavy tribute to Athens each year. But the city was full of Corinthians who were busy stirring up trouble. Late in 433, Pericles began to suspect that Potidaea was toying with the idea of rebelling against Athens.

He sent an ambassador to the Potidaeans, warning them

not to start trouble. Potidaea obediently promised to be loyal to Athens—but, at the suggestion of Corinth, secretly begged Sparta for help. Corinth, still stinging from her own defeat at the hands of Athens, urged the Spartans to go to the aid of Potidaea.

The Potidaeans grew more daring. The city buzzed with talk of rebellion. In June, 432, Pericles finally had to send an army to restore order.

An Athenian general named Archestratus was in command. He had 30 ships and 1,000 hoplites in his force, and one of those hoplites was a short, unattractive-looking man of thirty-eight, already well-known in Athens as some sort of philosopher—Socrates.

It was a grueling campaign. A Corinthian called Aristeus had rounded up a volunteer army of 2,000 soldiers from southern Greece, including some Spartans, and had gone to Potidaea's defense. Socrates and his fellow soldiers found themselves far from home, in a chilly part of Greece, fighting against an enemy stubbornly determined to break the power of Athens.

Socrates was not the only well-known Athenian who took part in the siege of Potidaea. Fighting alongside him was handsome, brilliant, dazzling Alcibiades, the darling of all Athens, a flamboyant and unpredictable character whose gaiety and dash were already legendary in Hellas.

Born around 450, Alcibiades was still in his teens when he fought at Potidaea. He came of aristocratic family; his father, Clinias, was of the important Eupatrid clan, while his mother was related to Pericles. Clinias was killed in battle when Alcibiades was three years old, and the boy grew up in the household of Pericles. Even when he was only a child, everyone seemed to sense that one day Alcibiades would lead Athens just as Pericles then did.

Alcibiades and Socrates were close friends. It was a friendship of opposites, for Alcibiades was everything that Socrates was not. He was good-looking and charming, while Socrates was plain and blunt-mannered. He was full of fun, given to pranks and wild escapades, whereas Socrates showed his sense of humor only in sly and ironic jokes. And Alcibiades was often drunk, unlike Socrates, who could drink the strong Greek wine all night without showing the slightest sign of unsteadiness.

Many years later, at a dinner party held in Athens, Alcibiades spoke of how Socrates had behaved during the long, grim siege at Potidaea. "His endurance was simply marvelous," Alcibiades remembered. "There were times when we were cut off from our supplies, and had to go without food. Nobody withstood hunger better than Socrates."

And his power to ignore bitter cold was also memorable. "There was a severe frost, for the winter up there is really frigid," Alcibiades said. "Anyone who went out had to wear a great quantity of clothes, and swaddle his feet in felt and fleeces. Yet, despite the cold, Socrates, with his bare feet on the ice and in his ordinary clothes, marched better than the other soldiers who had shoes. The others looked daggers at him, because they thought he was mocking them."

Alcibiades recalled another curious incident of the campaign that was typical of Socrates. One morning, said Alcibiades, Socrates began to contemplate some important problem of philosophy. "He stood still on the spot to consider it. When he couldn't solve it, he didn't give up, but stood there thinking from early dawn till noon."

Word began to pass among the other soldiers that Socrates had been standing in one place for hours, lost in thought. Some of them came over to stare at him, but Socrates took no more notice of them than if they had been invisible. "Finally," said Alcibiades, "in the evening after dinner, some Ionians brought their bedding outside—it was summertime—where they could take their rest in the cool and at the same time keep an eye on Socrates to see if he would stand there all night, as well. He remained standing until dawn. Then he made a prayer to the sun and went away."

The fighting at Potidaea was fierce and hot. Socrates was in the thick of things, and so was Alcibiades. When Alcibiades fell, wounded, Socrates rescued him, carrying him safely from the battlefield. After the battle, the Athenian generals came to Alcibiades to award him a decoration for bravery.

"No," he said. "The prize should go to Socrates."

But the generals declined to give Socrates the honor. They were more fond of Alcibiades, because of his important political connections and his wide popularity. Besides, Socrates himself had said he had no interest in medals. So the prize went to Alcibiades, despite his protest.

The Athenians were successful at Potidaea, and the army came home. Socrates went back to his usual pursuit, that of asking questions of people. But shadows were darkening over sunny Athens. The golden age of Pericles was near its end. The bloody events at Corcyra and Potidaea clearly indicated war would soon be at hand.

There was tension in Athens. As always, when war threatens, people become suspicious of one another. Every man is a potential enemy. Anyone who teaches strange things is in danger of being thought a security risk.

The Athens of the **great** years had been tolerant of new

ideas. Now, at the edge of war, that tolerance gave way. One of the victims of the new attitude was the philosopher Anaxagoras. He was a close adviser of Pericles, and many Athenians feared he might fill the leader's head with dangerous thoughts. Like anyone who has been in public life for many years, Pericles had acquired a number of enemies. They did not dare to attack Pericles, so they directed their fire at his friend and teacher, Anaxagoras.

The philosopher was brought to trial on a charge of "impiety." A special law was passed, making it a crime to fail to conform to the religious observances of the city, or to teach doctrines "concerning things in the sky." Anaxagoras had been arguing that the sun and the moon were not gods, but simply places like the earth. The moon, he said, had plains and valleys, and was inhabited.

The trumped-up charge was not really taken seriously, of course. What Anaxagoras' enemies actually were worried about was the rumor that the philosopher was scheming with the Persians against Athens. But that could not be proved while everyone knew of Anaxagoras' teachings about the sun and the moon. So Anaxagoras went on trial for impiety, and was sentenced to death. With the aid of Pericles, Anaxagoras was allowed to escape to the distant city of Lampsacus, where he founded a school and lived for many years thereafter. The Athenians were satisfied; they had not desired his death so much as simply to drive him far from Athens.

Socrates must have returned from Potidaea just in time to see his old teacher put on trial and then forced into exile. It could not have been pleasant to see how narrowminded the once-tolerant Athenians had become under the pressure of war. Certainly Socrates must have seen in the fate of Anaxagoras an omen for his own future. He was not popular in Athens. Would the time come when he, too, would be forced to choose between exile and death?

Another man, heeding the warning, might have changed his ways and given up his habit of asking troublesome questions. Not Socrates. He went his way, indifferent to any danger, just as though nothing at all had happened to Anaxagoras. He continued to plague people with his questions.

And war came nearer.

The city of Megara, which a few years before had been part of the empire of Athens, broke away and allied herself with Corinth. Athens tried to punish Megara by imposing an embargo: no city of the Delian League was allowed to do business with Megara. Corinth protested. Sparta entered the dispute and demanded that Athens lift the embargo. Pericles refused.

The Athenian leader suggested that the dispute be arbitrated under the terms of the Thirty Years' Peace.

"No," replied the Spartan ephor Sthenelaidas. "The Thirty Years' Peace is at an end. Sparta must stand by her friends." Hungry for war, the Spartans voted to attack Athens. One of history's most terrible wars was about to begin, the Peloponnesian War, which was destined to leave all Greece in ruins before its 30-year course was run. Sparta had remained idle while Athens grew mighty for, though they were great soldiers, the Spartans had a tradition of never going to war unless they were compelled to do so. Now they sought war.

Thucydides, the Greek historian who wrote the classic account of the Peloponnesian War, explained the position in these words: "The Athenians were growing too great to be ignored and were laying hands on Sparta's allies. The Spartans could now bear it no longer. They made up their

minds that they must put out all their strength and overthrow the Athenian power by force of arms. And therefore
they commenced the Peloponnesian War."

Sparta's first move was a bold one. A Spartan army
marched right into Attica and occupied the deme of
Acharnae, only six miles from Athens! The people of the
countryside fled within Athens' stout walls, while the invaders set fire to the rich vineyards and olive groves. The
Athenian army defended the area between Acharnae and
the city, but made no attempt to march against the Spartans. All summer long, the enemy rampaged near Athens.
Within the city, life went on almost as usual, though the
refugees from the countryside caused great overcrowding.
At the summer's end, the Spartans realized they could not
hope to get within striking distance of Athens, and they
withdrew, since Athenian ships were harassing the Pelo-
ponnesians in other parts of Greece.

The first year of the war had ended without any great
harm to Athens. But Athenians had died in defense of
their country, and late in 431 Athens held a great state
funeral for all the fallen soldiers.

Pericles delivered the funeral oration. It was a speech
designed to rally the morale of the Athenians, to keep
them on guard and ready for the struggles to come. Just as
an American President, delivering a Fourth of July speech
in wartime, might speak of the past greatness of the United
States, so did Pericles praise the accomplishments of
Athens.

"We are called a democracy," he said, "for the admin-
istration is in the hands of the many and not the few. No
man is barred from public service because of poverty or
low birth. Personal merit is the standard for which a citizen is distinguished."

He made some pointed remarks perhaps directed at the persecutors of Anaxagoras: "Our city is thrown open to the world, and we never expel a foreigner or prevent him from seeing or learning anything of which the secret if revealed to an enemy might profit him. We rely not upon management or trickery, but upon our own hearts and hands." He stressed Athens' traditional tolerance: "Not only in our public life are we liberal, but also as regards our freedom from suspicion of one another in the pursuits of everyday life; for we do not feel resentment at our neighbor if he does as he likes, nor yet do we put on sour looks which, though harmless, are painful to behold."

And, Pericles said, "We are lovers of the beautiful, yet simple in our tastes, and we cultivate the mind without loss of manliness. Wealth we employ rather as an opportunity for action than as a subject for boasting. With us it is no disgrace to be poor; the true disgrace is in doing nothing to avoid poverty."

He spoke of Athenian democracy: "We alone regard a man who takes no interest in public affairs, not as one who minds his own business, but as one who is good for nothing. We Athenians decide public questions for ourselves in open debate." He defended Athens against a charge of imperialism: "We alone do good to our neighbors not upon a calculation of interest, but in the confidence of freedom and in a frank and fearless spirit."

Summing up, Pericles called Athens "the school of Hellas." Each Athenian, he said, "in his own person seems to have the power of adapting himself to the most varied forms of action with the utmost versatility and grace. For in the hour of trial Athens alone among her contemporaries is superior."

It was a noble speech, an inspiring speech. But it might

well have been made in the past tense. Athens *had* been great. Now, locked in a savage war, Athens was undergoing change. Soon Pericles would be dead, and new men would guide the destinies of Athens. The war would take a tragic toll. Not merely lives would be lost, but the spirit of Athens itself—that spirit of open inquiry, of wise toleration—that had made the age of Pericles a golden age, indeed.

Certainly Pericles could foresee none of these events as he delivered his funeral oration. Perhaps few men in Athens were aware of the fate in store for their city. Perhaps none but Socrates, whose life now was past its halfway point, and who for so many years had painstakingly pursued truth in his own special way.

There was nothing Socrates could do to save Athens from her doom. He had offered his life in her military service, and he had tried to make her leaders wiser men. More than that he could not do.

4

❖ ❖ ❖

The Man of Many Questions

Socrates had experienced the golden years of Athens at
first hand. He had been born in Athens, in the deme of
Alopece, and he had hardly ever left his native city except
to serve in her armies. He did not even like to go beyond
the walls of Athens into the lovely countryside surrounding the city. One day, when he did go for a walk in the
country with a young friend named Phaedrus, Socrates
looked at the trees and the grass and the streams in awe
and surprise, as though he had never seen such things before. Phaedrus teased him for never leaving the city. "You
don't even go for so much as a stroll outside the walls,"
Phaedrus said.

"You must bear with me," Socrates replied. "I am so
fond of learning. Trees, you know, and fields, won't teach
me anything, but men in the city will."

We have already seen how, as a very young man, Socrates went round Athens to listen to the lectures of the

various philosophers. He heard this one and that, and noticed that they were all in conflict with each other, endlessly arguing about the nature of the world. He soon grew
tired of what they had to say. Even Anaxagoras, who for a
while impressed Socrates, eventually went off into woolly
realms of thought that left the young Athenian cold.

Why pry into the secrets of the heavens and the earth,
Socrates asked, when you are still ignorant of your own
soul? Why waste energy discussing the way the universe is
made, when it is much more important to know *why* it is
made the way it is? Questions of science did not attract
him. Questions of basic wisdom did.

Only nobody was teaching the things the young Socrates
wanted to know—and he did not think they could be
taught at all, anyway. He realized that he would have to be
his own teacher, to go around asking questions about justice and truth, about courage and righteousness, about
wisdom and virtue, until he was able to understand what
those terms meant.

One strange thing set Socrates apart from other men. He
had what he called a "divine sign," an inner voice which
guided him. "I have had it from childhood," he told the
men of Athens when he was on trial for his life. "It is a
kind of voice which, whenever I hear it, always turns me
back from something which I was going to do." It was an
odd kind of voice, never telling Socrates what he *should*
do, but only what he should *not* do.

Socrates heeded the sign whenever he felt it. Perhaps it
was his sign that turned him away from the babbling philosophers of Athens, and sent him out to seek truth in his
own way. Perhaps it was the sign that warned him not to
waste his time as a sculptor, when there were so many
important things for him to learn.

A different kind of divine voice also played a great part in the life of Socrates. This was the Oracle of Delphi, whose mysterious prophecies did much to influence Greek life 25 centuries ago.

Delphi was a sanctuary sacred to Apollo. There was a chasm in the earth at Delphi, through which strange, intoxicating gases rose from the depths. A splendid temple was erected above this chasm, and a priestess of Apollo occupied a three-legged chair directly over it. The vapors rising from the earth would throw her into a trance. Those who sought advice from Apollo would enter the temple and question the priestess. She would answer in enigmatic words that often did not mean quite what they seemed to mean.

The Oracle of Delphi was consulted by all who were in doubt. One who used the Oracle was Croesus, the astoundingly wealthy king of Lydia, in Asia Minor. About 550 B.C., Croesus was troubled by the growing power of Cyrus, King of Persia. He sent to Delphi a messenger, laden with gold and silver as gifts for the Oracle.

"Shall Croesus send an army against the Persians?" the messenger asked.

"If he does," the Oracle replied, "he will destroy a great empire."

Croesus was overjoyed. He attacked Cyrus at once, and his army was slaughtered. He himself became a prisoner of the Persian king. The Oracle, though, had spoken the truth. By attacking Cyrus, Croesus had indeed destroyed a great empire—his own.

So the tricky words of the Oracle had to be interpreted carefully.

When Socrates was still a young man, not even thirty years old, he found himself the center of a group of eager fellow students who were impressed by his wisdom and wanted to learn from him. In vain, Socrates protested that he had nothing to teach, that he was only a student himself. These friends of his clustered around him, hoping that some of his wisdom would rub off on them.

One of these early disciples of Socrates was a man named Chaerephon, a skinny, pale, awkward fellow who followed him around everywhere. Chaerephon believed that Socrates was the wisest man in Athens, and possibly in all the world. To prove it, Chaerephon made a journey to Delphi to consult the Oracle.

"Is there any man wiser than Socrates?" Chaerephon asked.

And the priestess replied, "There is no man wiser than Socrates."

Socrates was baffled and greatly disturbed when Chaerephon returned to Athens with his tidings. He knew all too well how deceptive the Oracle's words might be. Chaerephon, making the mistake of Croesus, had already taken the Oracle's answer at its face value. Obviously, Chaerephon argued, Socrates was the wisest man in the world!

Socrates himself was not so sure. "What can the god mean by this riddle?" he asked. "I know very well that I am not wise, even in the smallest degree. Then what can he mean by saying that I am the wisest of men?"

It could not be that the Oracle had lied, because the Oracle spoke with the voice of Apollo, and gods did not lie. For a long while, Socrates was at a loss to understand the meaning of the Oracle. Then he thought of a way to fathom the mystery.

He decided to look for a man who was obviously wiser than he was. When he had found him, he would go to Delphi and point out the Oracle's mistake, saying, "You said that I was the wisest of men, but this man is wiser than I am."

Socrates went first to an Athenian politician who was famous for his wisdom. He questioned him on many subjects. "When I conversed with him," Socrates said later, "I came to see that, though a great many persons, and most of all he himself, thought that he was wise, yet he was not wise."

Socrates tried to prove to the politician that he was not really wise, but only imagined himself wise. Naturally, the man quickly became angry, since Socrates was publicly exposing him as a fool. Socrates went away.

"I am wiser than this man," Socrates thought as he took his leave. "Neither of us knows anything that is really worthwhile, but he knows nothing and thinks that he knows; I neither know nor think that I know. At any rate, I seem to be a little wiser than he is on this point: I do not think that I know what I do not know."

He went on to another man, and another, to those who were most highly esteemed for their wisdom. The same thing happened every time. The so-called wise man was always sure of his wisdom at the beginning of the conversation. But as Socrates went on asking questions, the wise one became confused and started to contradict himself. Then he grew angry and stalked away from the man who had shown him up.

After he had talked to a great many of Athens' political leaders, Socrates began to see a disturbing thing: "I found that the men whose reputation for wisdom stood highest were nearly the most lacking in it, while others who were looked down on as common people were much more intelligent."

Still seeking a man wiser than himself, Socrates turned

now to the poets and playwrights. He studied their best works and questioned them, trying to find out what they had meant. "I am ashamed to tell you, my friends," Socrates said in later years, "but almost any bystander could have talked about the works of these poets better than the poets themselves." He discovered that poets wrote "by a certain natural power and by inspiration," not out of wisdom. Yet it seemed that a man who had written great poetry generally came to believe he was wise in all things, which Socrates found was not so.

Having had no luck with the poets, Socrates turned to the artisans—the men who worked with their hands, the stonemasons and pottery makers and other craftsmen. "I knew very well that I possessed no knowledge at all worth speaking of," he said, choosing to forget his own training as a stonemason. "And I was sure that I should find that they knew many fine things. And in that I was not mistaken. They knew what I did not know, and so far they were wiser than I. But it seemed to me that the skilled artisans had the same failing as the poets. Each of them believed himself to be extremely wise in matters of the greatest importance because he was skillful in his own art. But this was not so."

Socrates now began to see what the Oracle had meant. "No man is wiser than Socrates," the Oracle had declared. Yet Socrates knew he was not wise at all. The answer to the riddle was this: only the gods were wise, and human wisdom was worth little or nothing. The man who knew he knew nothing was the wisest of all, because he was not deluding himself.

Then, if none of us is wise, what could a man do?

He could go on asking, and trying to learn. The Oracle had declared, in effect, "He among you is the wisest who, like Socrates, knows that in truth his wisdom is worth nothing at all." So Socrates took it as a divine command to go among men, testing and questioning them. It would be his mission in life to expose the folly of those who thought themselves wise. In that way, by puncturing false pride and attacking false wisdom, Socrates hoped he could help some men to reach real wisdom. And he hoped he would grow wiser himself in the process.

Now he began to go around Athens in earnest, every day, doing nothing but engaging people in conversation and trying to make them see how confused and contradictory their opinions really were. "He was always in public view," wrote Xenophon, a friend of Socrates, in his *Memoirs*. "In the morning he went to the arcades and gymnasiums; when the market place filled he was to be seen there, and the rest of the day you might find him wherever the most people were to be met. He was generally talking, and anyone might listen."

Yet Socrates did not give long lectures, the way other philosophers did. He had no answers, only questions. As Xenophon put it:

"He did not even discuss that topic so favored by other talkers, 'the Nature of the Universe,' and avoided speculation on the so-called 'Cosmos' of the professors, how it works, and on the laws that govern the phenomena of the heavens: indeed he would argue that to trouble one's mind with such problems is sheer folly. His own conversation was ever of human things. The problems he discussed were, What is godly, what is ungodly; what is beautiful, what is ugly; what is just, what is unjust; what is prudence, what is madness; what is courage, what is cowardice; what is government, and what is a governor."

The way in which he discussed these matters—the so-

called *Socratic method*—was always the same. We have already seen Socrates use his method on Euthyphro, in a
discussion of piety and impiety. It consisted of asking questions around a central theme. Socrates never openly said,
when one of his questions was answered, "That is wrong."
He would simply say, "Let us see if that is correct," and ask
more questions. Step by step, he would lead his companion
on, until the answerer himself saw the glaring contradictions of his words. Always, when he conducted such an
inquiry, Socrates was polite, patient, even apologetic.
There was always humor in his manner, too. He pretended
to be a simple man, a humble inquirer after truth, who did
not himself know the answers to his questions. This mock
humility was a trademark of his, the well-known Socratic
irony.

The method of Socrates is known as *dialectic,* the
method of "conversation." He felt that truth could only be
reached through a dialogue, or debate, between two speak-
ers. The point toward which a dialectic inquiry aimed was
known as an *elenchos,* or refutation—the point at which
one party came to see that the idea he was defending was
incorrect or confused.

Elenchos had an older meaning to the Greeks: disgrace,
dishonor. A man refuted by his own words felt disgraced
and dishonored. Some men were big enough to admit that
they had profited by their elenchos at the hands of Socrates; others simply became angry at him for showing them
up.

Certain Athenians realized how valuable Socrates was,
and they sought out his company, deliberately engaging in
conversation with him. He sharpened their wits in discussion after discussion, so that eventually they were almost
able to hold their own with him. Socrates relished the

company of these friends. He once said, so Xenophon wrote, that "a good friend gives me the same pleasure as a good horse, or dog, or gamecock gives another man, or even more. If I know anything good, I teach it to my friends, and introduce them to others from whom I think they will profit in goodness. I join with my friends in unrolling the treasures of the wits of old times, which they have left behind them in written scrolls, and if we find a good thing there, we pick it out, and think we have won great gain if we become friends."

Another friend of Socrates, Plato, contradicts this statement to some extent. Plato makes Socrates hostile to written books. In a work of Plato's called *Phaedrus,* Socrates is quoted as calling writing "evil," because a book cannot be part of a discussion. Looking at books, Socrates says, "You could fancy they speak as though they were possessed of sense, but if you wish to understand something they say, and question them about it, you find them ever repeating but one and the selfsame story."

Certainly Socrates himself had no interest in writing books. He never set a word of his thinking down on paper. Luckily for us, his pupil Plato devoted many years of his life to writing what he called *Socratic dialogues,* which recorded some of Socrates' conversations. The earliest of Plato's dialogues were written right after Socrates died, and so they probably reflect the ideas of Socrates nearly in his actual words. Later, Plato wrote Socratic dialogues in which Socrates appeared almost as a fictional character, speaking Plato's own thoughts. When we read Plato, we have to stop and consider where the character of Socrates is speaking for himself and where he is just a mouthpiece for the younger philosopher, Plato, whose ideas sometimes were quite different from his master's.

In order to devote himself entirely to his new life of asking questions, Socrates had to give up any thought of earning a living. He took upon himself that poverty which Pericles, in his funeral oration, said was no disgrace. He lived on the money his father had left him, and did without all luxuries.

He lived so simply that another philosopher, Antiphon, once said to him, "You are living a life that would drive even a slave to desert his master. Your meat and drink are of the poorest; the cloak you wear is not only a poor thing, but is never changed summer or winter; and you never wear shoes or tunic."

"But," replied Socrates, "my belief is that to have no wants is divine; to have as few as possible comes next to the divine."

One problem created by Socrates' decision to spend all his time in conversation was the support of his family. For Socrates had acquired a wife named Xanthippe. He probably married her when he was thirty-five or even forty; that is, after the Oracle of Delphi had spoken. We think so because, when Socrates was seventy, the oldest of his three children was only about eighteen.

Xanthippe has become proverbial for her bad temper. No doubt she found it extremely trying to live with a philosopher like Socrates, who was so busy discussing justice and virtue that he had no time to earn a living. One story about her tells of the time when Socrates was lost in one of his famous meditations, standing stock-still and paying no attention to anything going on around him. Xanthippe wanted to tell him something important, and she hopped up and down in front of him, scolding and shouting at him.

Socrates apparently took no notice. Finally, Xanthippe

picked up a bucket of dirty water and flung it over him. Socrates simply smiled and said mildly, "It generally rains after thunder."

There are many other tales of Xanthippe's shrewishness, and perhaps most of them were invented long after Socrates' time. Plato, who knew Socrates and wrote more about him than anyone else, nowhere talks of Xanthippe's bad temper. The only time she appears as a character in one of Plato's works, she is shown as an affectionate and loving wife.

Xenophon, who also wrote dialogues in which Socrates appears as a character, makes Socrates give this explanation for his marriage to Xanthippe:

"I see," Socrates said, "that those who wish to become skillful horsemen get the most spirited horses rather than the gentlest. For they suppose that if they can bridle these, they will be able to deal with any horse. So I, wishing to mingle among men and deal with them, have married this woman, knowing well that if I can endure *her*, I can easily get along with anyone at all."

5

❖ ❖ ❖

Socrates and the Sophists

Socrates was not the only thoughtful Greek who had turned away from matters of natural science. A whole school of philosophers had emerged, around 450 B.C., to study the same things that interested Socrates: the personal conduct of life, the principles of law and morality, the nature of man's relation to his polis.

These men were called sophists. The word means "teacher of *sophia,*" and *sophia* had a complicated meaning combining the ideas of "wisdom," "cleverness" and "practical ability." Today, "sophist" is a word of accusation. When we say a man is a sophist, we mean that he is a glib and cynical talker who distorts the truth to prove whatever point he wants to put across. It had no such meaning in ancient Athens. A sophist was simply a kind of professor who taught *sophia.*

Though the topics they dealt with were the same as

those of Socrates, the methods of the sophists were altogether different. For one thing, they took fees. They traveled from city to city, giving lectures on various subjects.
For a fixed sum, a sophist would hold forth on such topics
as "How to conduct one's private affairs well" or "What is
good poetry?" or "How can a man best serve his polis."

Another difference was the way they taught. They gave
standard lectures and did not encourage questions from
the audience. Socrates gave no lectures at all, and depended entirely on questions and answers. He did not even
claim to be a teacher, while the sophists boasted of their
learning and wisdom and of their ability to improve the
minds of others.

There were many of these sophists, and they all earned a
good living in Athens, where everyone was eager to learn.
Some of the sophists were foolish and empty-headed;
others were profound thinkers of great intellect. But Socrates had no use for any of the sophists, neither the good
ones nor the bad. To his way of thinking, they were all
equally harmful.

Socrates disliked the sophists because they tended to
keep men from doing their own thinking. For Socrates,
wisdom was not attained by standing openmouthed before
a Great Mind who expounded his Great Thoughts. Wisdom could only be attained—if at all—by patient search
and hard work. So even the finest of the sophists earned the
disapproval of Socrates.

Then, too, there were the quack sophists, slick, fast-
talking peddlers of learning who could twist an argument
in any direction to suit their own purposes. Some of these
sophists even used Socrates' own question-and-answer
method, not to find truth but to hide it.

One of Plato's dialogues, *Euthydemus,* shows two such

sophists in action. They were brothers, Euthydemus and Dionysodorus, who had come from the Ionian city of Chios to teach in Athens. "Such is their skill in the war of words," Socrates said of them with sarcasm, "that they can refute any proposition whether true or false."

Socrates went to visit the newcomers. With typical irony, he pretended that he was hopeful of learning wisdom from them. When he came upon them at the open-air gymnasium where most Athenians spent at least part of every day in exercise and discussion, the two sophists were already in debate with two well-bred Athenian youths, Cleinias and Ctesippus. When Socrates arrived and joined the group, he asked the sophists what it was they taught.

"The teaching of virtue, Socrates, is our principal occupation," replied Euthydemus. "And we believe that we can impart it better and quicker than any man."

For a while, Socrates let the sophists play their tricks on him. Then he drew Cleinias aside, and tried to explain to the young man just what was going on. However, Cleinias was under the spell of the sophists. He believed firmly that wisdom could be taught. So Socrates stepped back a pace, and watched in amusement as Euthydemus and Dionysodorus juggled words and dazzled Cleinias and Ctesippus.

Dionysodorus set out to prove that Ctesippus' dog was also Ctesippus' father.

"You say you have a dog?" the sophist asked.

"Yes," Ctesippus replied, "a villain of one."

"And he has puppies?"

"Yes, and they are very like himself."

"And the dog is the father of them?" Dionysodorus asked.

"Yes, certainly he is."

"And the dog is yours?"

"To be sure he is."

"Then he is a father, and he is yours. Therefore, he is your father, and the puppies are your brothers."

Ctesippus shook his head in confusion at this triumph of sophistry. How could his dog be his father? His dog was *a* father, all right, the father of puppies. But—but—

While Ctesippus tried to figure it out, the sophist slipped in one last thrust. "Do you beat this dog?" he asked.

"Indeed, I do," said Ctesippus, laughing. "And I only wish I could beat you instead of him."

"Then you beat your father," the sophist said.

Now Socrates rejoined the discussion, and the sophists, using their mockery of the Socratic method, proved all sorts of absurd things the same way. Socrates good-naturedly went along with the fun, and even applauded their wit. He praised the sophists with ironic words, leaving no doubt in the minds of the onlookers that he regarded their "wisdom" as mere tomfoolery and bamboozlement.

On another occasion, Socrates had an encounter with a much more respectable sophist, Protagoras of Abdera. The meeting took place a few years before the outbreak of the Peloponnesian War—perhaps about 435 B.C. Socrates was thirty-five then, and just beginning to make a reputation for himself as a man of deep and original thought.

Protagoras was a sophist of enormous prestige. He was then about fifty years old, and had traveled all over Greece, lecturing in many cities and drawing great crowds. His fees were high, and he had become a wealthy man simply through his lecture tours. Now he was visiting Athens again, staying in the home of the rich man, Callias.

Socrates had no particular interest in meeting this best-known and wisest of sophists. Every important man in

Athens had gone to the home of Callias to pay homage to Protagoras. He had been in town for two days, but Socrates had not gone. Quite early on the third morning, Socrates was awakened by a great thumping on his door. It was Hippocrates, one of Socrates' friends (who is not to be confused with Hippocrates of Cos, the great Greek doctor of the same era).

"Socrates, are you awake or asleep?" Hippocrates bellowed.

"Do you bring any news?" Socrates answered.

"Good news, nothing but good."

"Delightful," Socrates said. "But what is the news? And why have you come here at this unearthly hour?"

"Protagoras is come," Hippocrates said solemnly.

"Yes, I know. He came two days ago. Have you only just heard of his arrival?"

Yes, Hippocrates said; he had learned yesterday evening that Protagoras was in Athens, and staying with Callias. And he urged Socrates to come with him at once to see Protagoras. He yearned for the wisdom that Protagoras could impart.

"Why are you so excited?" Socrates asked. "Has Protagoras done you any harm?"

"Yes, he has," Hippocrates said with a laugh. "He keeps his wisdom to himself, and does not make me wise."

"But I have no doubt," said Socrates, "that if you only give him money enough, he will make you wise too."

But it was too early to go. Socrates suggested that he and Hippocrates stroll about the courtyard until dawn, and talk a while. Hippocrates agreed. He talked eagerly of paying money to Protagoras and becoming his disciple.

"But are you aware of the danger you are incurring?" Socrates asked. "If you were going to commit your body to someone who might do good or harm to it, would you not carefully consider and ask the opinion of your friend and kindred, and deliberate many days as to whether you should give him the care of your body?"

"Of course, Socrates."

"But when the soul is in question—which you hold to be of far more value than the body—about this you never consulted either with your father or your brother or with any one of us who are your companions. No sooner does this foreigner appear than you instantly commit your soul to his keeping."

Then Socrates compared a sophist to a tradesman: "Is not a sophist, Hippocrates, one who deals wholesale or retail in the food of the soul?"

"And what, Socrates, is the food of the soul?"

"Surely," he said, "knowledge is the food of the soul. And we must take care, my friend, that the sophist does not deceive us when he praises what he sells, like the dealers who sell the foods of the body. For these dealers are ignorant, and praise everything they sell, whether it is good or bad for the body."

"And a sophist?" Hippocrates asked.

"It is exactly the same. Those who hawk about their wares of knowledge from city to city, selling them to any customer who comes forward, praise their whole stock alike. But some of these, too, my good friend, may very likely be unable to tell us which of their wares is good and which bad for the soul, unless he who buys of them happens to be skilled in the medicine of the soul. If then you are skilled in these matters, and can say which is good and which is bad, there is no danger in your buying instructions from Protagoras, or any other person whatever. But if not, then have a care, my good Hippocrates, that you do not stake and imperil your dearest treasure."

Having warned Hippocrates to be wary of sophists, Socrates then agreed to pay a call on Protagoras. Together, they went to the house of Callias and knocked at the door. The doorkeeper came out, obviously bothered by the high-flown discussions that had been going on in his master's house for the last two days.

"What? More sophists!" the porter exclaimed. "The master is busy!" And he slammed the door in the faces of Socrates and Hippocrates.

Again they knocked, and this time managed to persuade the man to let them in. They found Protagoras taking a walk in the courtyard of the house, with a crowd of disciples surrounding him. Callias was there, of course, and Paralus, a son of Pericles, and Charmides, uncle of Plato. (Plato had not been born when this encounter took place.) Elsewhere in the room, Socrates saw Xanthippus, another son of Pericles, and dozens of others who had come to hear Protagoras. Alcibiades was there, too, though only in his middle teens.

Socrates was amused by the way this great crowd of disciples followed Protagoras up and down the courtyard. Everyone clustered close, to hear each precious word. "I was delighted by the precision of their movements," Socrates later said to a friend to whom he described the meeting. "They never got in his way at all. The moment the great master and his party turned, then the band of listeners deftly and daintily turned off to the right and left, and, wheeling round, took their places behind him in the prettiest order."

It was quite different from the style of Socrates, who met

his friends face to face. Protagoras was "followed," not only figuratively but literally.

Socrates, not at all awed by the distinguished visitor, went straight up to him. "Protagoras, my friend Hippocrates and I have come to see you."

"Do you wish to speak to me alone, or in the presence of the company?"

"Whichever you please," Socrates answered, and soon a discussion was under way. Socrates opened the debate by asking Protagoras what sort of instruction Hippocrates could expect if he became the sophist's pupil. Protagoras replied that he taught men how to be good citizens.

"I wish that you would, if possible, show me how virtue can be taught," Socrates asked innocently.

Protagoras replied by delivering a long speech. Sidestepping Socrates' troublesome questions, he spoke for many minutes, making a grand and noble oration, using the great artfulness for which he was famous. His words were ringing and well chosen, and Socrates found himself being lulled by the rhythms of the sophist's voice, so that he was not really paying attention to the actual ideas Protagoras was putting forth.

When Protagoras had finished, Socrates praised him for his eloquence. Many orators, he said, could make a fine speech, however. "But then, when one has a question to ask of any of them, like books they can neither answer nor ask. And if anyone challenges the least particular of their speech, they go ringing on in a long harangue, like brazen pots, which when they are struck continue to sound unless some one puts his hand on them."

Slyly, Socrates went on to say that he was sure Protagoras was not one of these "brazen pots." Surely the sophist would not mind engaging in some question-and-answer discussion now, and would make brief answers to Socrates' brief questions?

Protagoras agreed to let himself be questioned. Socrates thereupon began to ask him about virtue and justice and wisdom. Before long, the distinguished sophist found himself tangled in a net of contradictions. He began to get irritated. Socrates was making him look foolish in front of dozens of his disciples! That would never do, for Protagoras had to think of his fees, which he would not earn if word got around that Socrates had humiliated him in debate.

So he attempted what we might call a filibuster. Instead of going on with the questioning, Protagoras made another lengthy speech, so eloquent that all his disciples burst out cheering when he had finished.

Only Socrates was unimpressed. "Protagoras," he said, "I have a wretched memory, and when anyone makes a long speech to me I never remember what he is talking about. I will ask you to cut your answers shorter, if you would take me with you."

"What do you mean? How am I to shorten my answers? Shall I make them too short?"

"Certainly not," Socrates said.

"But short enough?"

"Yes."

"Shall I answer what appears to me to be short enough, or what appears to you to be short enough?"

Socrates suggested that Protagoras decide that for himself. The sophist replied that he was uncomfortable about fighting this battle of words with the methods of Socrates. He preferred his own way of debate, at which he was a champion.

"I don't wish to force the conversation upon you if you

had rather not," Socrates answered evenly. "But when you're willing to argue with me in such a way that I can follow you, then I will argue with you." Since Protagoras insisted on making speeches instead of making brief interchanges of conversation, Socrates said he would take his leave.

As he rose to go, Callias, the host, caught his cloak. "We cannot let you go, Socrates," he said. "There is nothing in the world I should like better than to hear you and Protagoras discourse. Do not deny our company this pleasure."

Socrates let himself be coaxed into staying. Since Protagoras only grew ruffled and excited when Socrates did the questioning, Socrates suggested a change of method: let Protagoras ask questions, and he would try to answer. Reluctantly, the sophist agreed to this, though he would much rather have made speeches.

Protagoras decided to get away from the topic of virtue, and to talk about poetry instead. He picked a passage from the poet Simonides, and began to question Socrates about it, using methods not very different from those by which Dionysodorus was able to prove that the father of Ctesippus was a dog. Almost at once, he managed to lead Socrates into contradicting himself.

The audience cheered as Protagoras scored a point. "I felt at first giddy and faint," Socrates later related, "as if I had received a blow from the hand of an expert boxer, when I heard his words and the sound of the cheering."

Soon, though, Socrates managed to pull himself out of his difficulty. He was able to show that Protagoras was merely playing with words, and that the contradiction he claimed to find in Socrates' answer did not really exist, any more than Ctesippus was really the brother of puppies.

Then, by way of having some fun with the older man, Socrates borrowed Protagoras' own favorite method, and proceeded to launch into a speech of his own! It was a long, flowery discussion of poetry, imitating all the tricks and cleverness of Protagoras. Protagoras, the wise and famous professor, must have held his temper with difficulty as the Athenian upstart with the comically ugly face mocked him so wittily.

When he had finished, Socrates suggested that they "have done with poems," and go back to the basic discussion about virtue. To argue about poetry, Socrates said, could be very entertaining, but it was nothing more than a time-passing amusement. "Leaving the poets, and keeping to ourselves," he said, "let us try the mettle of one another and make proof of the truth in conversation."

Protagoras, growing more and more disturbed by all this, found that he had been trapped. If he refused to debate with Socrates, he would look like a coward in front of all his disciples. So, after grumbling a little, he agreed to resume the discussion of virtue. Socrates could ask questions, and he would answer.

Socrates thanked Protagoras for his cooperation. "Don't imagine," he said, "that I have any other interest in asking questions of you but that of clearing up my own difficulties. And I would rather converse with you than with anyone, because I think no one understands these matters as well as you."

Soothed by the flattery, Protagoras readied himself for a new barrage of questions. Socrates began to ask about virtue and bravery. They had left a question unanswered before: "Are wisdom and temperance and courage and justice and holiness five names of the same thing, or are they each separate things?"

Protagoras now answered, "All these qualities are parts of virtue. And one of them, courage, is different from the other four. A man can be utterly ignorant, intemperate, unjust and unholy, and still be remarkable for his courage."

"Stop," said Socrates. "I should like to think about that. When you speak of brave men, do you mean the confident?"

"Yes. I mean those who are ready to go at that which others are afraid to approach."

"And you say that virtue is a good thing? And bravery, being a part of virtue, is also good?"

"Yes," Protagoras said. "I should say it is the best of all things—wholly good, in the highest degree."

Socrates spoke softly as he closed in on the sophist. "Tell me then: who are they who have confidence when diving in a well?"

"I should say, the divers."

"And they are confident because they have knowledge?"

"Yes, that is the reason."

"And who have confidence when fighting on horseback, the skilled horsemen or the unskilled?"

"The skilled," Protagoras said. "It is true in all things. Those who have knowledge are more confident than those who have no knowledge, and they are more confident after they have learned than before."

"And," said Socrates, "have you never seen an ignorant person full of confidence?"

"Many times."

"And are not these confident persons also courageous?"

"In that case," said Protagoras, "courage would be a base thing, for those men are surely madmen."

"Then those who are confident without knowledge are

really not courageous, but mad. In that case the wisest are also the most confident, and being the most confident, are also the bravest. And so wisdom is courage."

It seemed that Protagoras was in trouble again; just a few moments before, he had said that a man could have courage without any of the other virtues. Now here was Socrates, proving that a man who had courage without wisdom had no courage at all, but was simply a madman! Protagoras complained that Socrates was twisting his words into strange meanings. Politely, Socrates suggested that they try to continue, and perhaps everything would come clear.

They went on, Socrates still following one theme: what is virtue? Is it one thing, or are all the virtues different from one another? Is there an *idea* of virtue, which includes all the different virtues of courage, wisdom, piety, and the rest? Round and round went the discussion, and Protagoras got more confused as Socrates mildly showed him all the inconsistencies and flaws in his thinking. Eventually they came back to the discussion of whether, as Protagoras said, a man could be ignorant and still courageous.

Socrates peppered Protagoras with questions. Eventually Protagoras refused to answer a question.

"Why do you say neither yes nor no, Protagoras?"

"Finish the argument by yourself," Protagoras said glumly.

"I only want to ask one more question. I want to know whether you still think that there are men who are most ignorant and yet most courageous?"

Weary, thoroughly defeated, the sophist threw in the towel. "You seem to have a great ambition to make me answer, Socrates. Very well: I admit it. This appears to me to be impossible, consistent with your line of argument."

Socrates smiled as he pointed out an odd thing: during the long debate, he and Protagoras had shifted sides! Socrates had started by saying that virtue could not be taught, but he had proved that virtue was knowledge, and so presumably could be taught. And Protagoras, who started by saying that virtue could be taught, was now eager to prove that it was anything but knowledge, in which case it could not be taught.

"Our ideas are in terrible confusion," Socrates said. "I have a great desire that they should be cleared up." He proposed that they start all over and search for the point where they had shifted sides.

But Protagoras had had enough. He earned his living by teaching virtue, and now Socrates had made him seem to say that virtue could not be taught. He did not care to risk his reputation any further. "Let us come back to the subject at some future time," he suggested. "At present, we had better turn to something else."

It had been a memorable morning for Socrates. He had met the famous Protagoras in debate, and had trounced him soundly. No doubt all Athens was abuzz with the details of the encounter before nightfall.

Embarrassed though he was, Protagoras showed his true nobility of spirit as Socrates prepared to leave. "I am the last man in the world to be envious," he said. "I applaud your energy and your conduct of an argument, Socrates. As I have often said, I admire you above all the men I know, and far above all men of your own age. And I go farther than that. I would not be surprised, Socrates, if you were to become one of the world's famous sages."

The conversation ended with this, and Socrates went his way.

6

❖ ❖ ❖

Athens at War

WHEN SOCRATES had debated with Protagoras, Athens was still enjoying peace. Yet the drums of war were beginning to pound in Hellas, and those golden days were nearly at their end.

In another two years, trouble broke out at Corcyra, and then, in 432, at Potidaea. As we have already seen, Socrates was among those citizens of Athens who went off to fight at Potidaea, and he served his polis well, fighting bravely despite the severe cold and the great dangers.

As a loyal Athenian, Socrates made no objections about being drafted. What did it matter that he was almost forty years old, or that it was more convenient for him to stay home and spend his time in pleasant discussion? Off he went. But when he came home, he lost no time returning to his old life. The very day he returned to Athens, he went to the gymnasium to find his friends. No sooner did he enter than he was hailed by everyone, and Chaerephon in particular came running up, seizing his hand.

"How did you escape, Socrates?"

"You see that I am here," he said simply.

"We heard the fighting was fierce, and many of our friends had fallen."

"True," Socrates said. He sat down and spoke for a few moments about the progress of the war. Then, as though he had not been gone at all, he fell right away into a philosophical discussion with young Charmides, who had been only a boy when Socrates left for Potidaea, but who now was a handsome young man.

And Socrates went on, talking with anyone who cared to debate with him, while disaster closed in on Athens. In 431 B.C., the year after his return from Potidaea, war began with Sparta. The Athenians held the enemy at bay the first year, a year that closed with the magnificent funeral oration of Pericles. But in 430 the Spartans invaded Attica again. Thousands of refugees from the outlying demes poured into Athens. And a frightful thing happened: in the overcrowded city, stifling in summer heat, a terrible plague broke out.

It began first in the Piraeus, the port of Athens, and spread to the main city. No one knew what had caused it, though some whispered that the Spartans had poisoned the wells. The doctors could do nothing; the plague spread from house to house, killing Athenians by the thousands.

One plague victim who recovered was Thucydides, the historian. He set down an unforgettable description of the grim malady. First came headache and redness of the eyes, he wrote, and then sneezing and hoarseness, followed by coughing and vomiting. The body was not warm to the touch, said Thucydides, "but internally it was consumed by such a heat that the patients could not bear to have on them the lightest coverings or linen sheets, but wanted to be quite uncovered and would have liked best to throw themselves into cold water—indeed, many of those who were not looked after did throw themselves into cisterns, so tormented were they by thirst which could not be quenched."

Most of the victims died on the seventh or the ninth day, worn out by the ravages of the disease. Of those who survived, some lost their memories, and could not recognize their friends or relatives, while others went blind, or lost their fingers and toes. Bodies lay unburied everywhere. The city was demoralized.

Socrates was in Athens during the time of the plague. We do not know whether he fell ill or not. In any event, he lived, and probably did all he could to care for the sufferers. Others were not so fortunate. The eldest son of Pericles died, and then Pericles' sister. Then a younger son of Pericles died also, and the aging leader did something he had never done before: he wept in public, as he put a wreath on the boy's grave. All told, nearly a third of the population of Athens perished from the plague.

The city was full of corpses, and the outlying demes were full of Spartan soldiers. The Athenians grew desperate and talked of begging for peace. There was no plague in Sparta, after all. Were the gods angry with Athens? Had Athens offended them by growing too proud?

And now the Athenians turned against Pericles. It was he who had made Athens great. Perhaps he was the one who had brought the anger of the gods against her. They shook their fists at him in rage. He warned them to save their energies for fighting the Spartans. This was a war

Athens could not afford to lose, for if she did, her enemies would destroy her. "The empire you hold is a tyranny, which it may seem wrong to have assumed, but which certainly it is dangerous to let go," Pericles declared.

He could not calm them. They brought him to trial on a charge of embezzlement, claiming he had stolen money from the city treasury and used it for his own private enrichment. In the hysteria of the moment, he was found guilty, fined, and deprived of his rights as a citizen.

A few months later, in the spring of 429, the Athenians repented. They restored Pericles to citizenship and made him their leader again. It was too late. He was a broken man, wounded by the campaign against his honesty, and saddened by the death of his sons and many of his friends. Soon he, too, fell ill of the plague, and by the summer he was dead. He had led Athens for more than 30 years, and now, in the time of her greatest trial, there was no leader to take his place. Other men, lesser men, struggled with one another to assume the leadership.

The war went on. It was a terrible war, in which the ideas of justice and virtue that had been so important to Hellas were quickly forgotten. Violence led to more violence. The city of Plataea, one of Athens' oldest allies, fell into Spartan hands, surrendering after getting a promise of just treatment. Then the Spartans slaughtered every man in the city, after holding a "trial" so the Plataeans could say they had been treated with justice.

Perhaps such cruelty might be expected of the grim Spartans. Athens, though, had a reputation for tolerance and mercy. Soon the Athenians were behaving no better than Spartans. In 428, Mitylene, a town of the League of Delos, revolted against Athens and turned to Sparta for help. A party of aristocrats took control of the town. Then there was an uprising against the rebels; a democratic faction gave the city back to Athens. The aristocrats surrendered and asked Athens for mercy.

One of the new leaders of Athens was Cleon, a tanner of hides, who had grown wealthy and powerful. A harsh, violent man, Cleon urged punishment for Mitylene as a lesson to the rest of the League: death for every man of Mitylene, slavery for the women and children. The Assembly voted and passed the decree. But the terrible vengeance was not carried out; at the last moment, the Athenians remembered that they were Athenians, and spared the lives of the people of Mitylene.

The struggle between aristocrats and democrats was going on all over Greece. The rich noblemen of each town supported Sparta in the war; the democratic merchants and shippers were backers of Athens. In 427, a year after the Mitylene incident, civil war broke out in Corcyra between aristocrats and democrats. This was the city that had first drawn Hellas into conflict, six years before. Now it suffered the worst agony that a polis could endure: men of Corcyra lifted weapons against other men of Corcyra. The pro-Athenian democrats massacred the pro-Spartan aristocrats, and then the aristocrats, gaining the upper hand, slaughtered the democrats. Thucydides put down this chilling report:

"Death in every form ensued, and whatever horrors are wont to be perpetrated at such times all happened then—aye, and even worse. For father slew son, men were dragged from the temples and slain near them, and some were even walled up in the temple of Dionysus and perished there."

And, Thucydides wrote in dismay, words lost their meaning in Corcyra. Wise hesitation was looked upon as cowardice. Reckless audacity was thought to be courage. Moderation was scorned as weakness. To Socrates of Athens, who put such store in the real meaning of words, the wild upheaval in Corcyra must have been sorrowful news. Something nightmarish was happening to Greece.

Up and down the land the armies raged. Now Athens took the initiative, and now it was Sparta that charged on to victory. Cities were destroyed; whole populations were swallowed up in slavery, or put to the sword. An earthquake struck Sparta, evening the score for Athens' plague, and giving the Athenians a chance to gather their strength. It was a confusing war, fought on many fronts at once.

The year 425 saw the Athenians definitely on the rise. Athens had always been matchless as a naval power; and after having fought Sparta on land for six years, the Athenians had learned enough about land combat from their enemies to meet them as equals in the field. Sparta, too, was troubled by the threat of a revolt of the helots, who saw the turmoil of war as a good chance to gain their own freedom. The Spartans began to think of negotiating a peace, calling off the war before more damage was done.

The Athenians were not minded to have peace. They were optimistic now, tasting victory at last after the shock of early defeat. They brushed aside the Spartan peace ambassadors, and went on fighting. Athens dreamed now of destroying Sparta completely, and establishing a land empire in Hellas as great as the seacoast empire she already possessed.

An important part of the Athenian strategy involved getting control of the inland city of Delium, north of Athens. Delium would serve as a base from which the Athenian armies could strike at the other cities in that part of Greece.

A Greek general named Hippocrates, who was neither the famous doctor nor the friend of Socrates and admirer of Protagoras, led an army of 7,000 hoplites and 1,000 cavalrymen to capture Delium. Socrates was one of the hoplites in that army although, in that year of 424, he was forty-six years old. Alcibiades was there, too, in the cavalry.

The Athenians seized Delium easily. But then came word that a vast army from Boeotia, an ally of Sparta, was on the way to drive the Athenians out of Delium.

Hippocrates left 300 cavalrymen to hold Delium, and marched out to confront the Boeotians. The two armies met about a mile south of Delium, late on a November afternoon in 424. At first, the Athenians did well, driving the enemy back despite the greater numbers of the Boeotians. But then a wing of cavalrymen from the city of Thebes moved around under cover of a hill, and slipped back of the Athenian right wing.

The Athenians, seeing them suddenly appear, thought that a whole new army was upon them. They panicked and fled. The Boeotians charged triumphantly, cutting the Athenian lines to shreds. Hippocrates was killed, and another general named Laches took command and tried desperately to rally the Athenian troops.

To no avail. A thousand of Athens' best hoplites died in the slaughter. Laches gave the signal for retreat, but it was a signal that did not need to be given, for the Athenian army was already in disorderly flight, running helter-skelter to safety.

One soldier who did not panic during the retreat was Socrates. After the rout began, Alcibiades and some other cavalrymen came upon Socrates, marching along next to Laches as they left the battlefield.

"I noticed that Socrates was far cooler than Laches,"

Alcibiades told some friends a few years later. "He was walking just the way he does in Athens, strutting along with his head in the air and casting sidelong glances. He was quietly watching both friend and foe, and making it perfectly plain, even from a distance, that anybody who attacked him would get a tough fight. That's how both he and Laches got off safe. Those who show a bold front in war are never touched; the ones who are running away headlong are those who are pursued."

Laches, too, had high praise for Socrates. "He was my companion in the retreat from Delium," he remarked to a friend in Athens, "and I can tell you that if others had only been like him, the honor of our country would have been upheld, and the great defeat would never have occurred."

But the defeat *had* occurred. Furthermore, a brilliant new Spartan general named Brasidas had revived Spartan morale. With a small but devoted band of soldiers, Brasidas had won several smashing victories. The tide of the war began to turn once again, now in Sparta's favor. In 423, Brasidas captured the important city of Amphipolis, on the northern coast of the Aegean Sea.

The fall of Amphipolis was a disaster for Athens. From the forests surrounding the city came the timber for Athenian ships. From the rich mines of Amphipolis came the gold and silver to pay the crushing expenses of the war. And by taking Amphipolis, the Spartans were in a position to cut off the all-important supplies of grain that reached Athens from the lands bordering the Black Sea to the east.

Brasidas, wiser than most Spartan generals, was treating the cities he had captured with moderation instead of brutality. He was winning many friends to the Spartan cause. Several of Athens' mainland possessions revolted and handed themselves over to Sparta. Only a couple of years before, the Athenians had scented total victory; now, with Brasidas taking the field against them, they feared defeat.

They asked for a one-year truce. That would give them a chance to work out a strategy that might defeat Brasidas. The Spartans were willing enough to grant the truce. They had already made great gains in the war, and they hoped that the truce might harden into a permanent peace that would leave them in control of the cities they had won.

So there was a rest from war, for the moment. Socrates returned to Athens and went back to his accustomed ways. But his homecoming was not altogether pleasant. He found himself the subject of a violent and unfair attack. It was the hardest kind of attack to deal with, too, because the weapon used against him was the invincible weapon of humor.

7

❖ ❖ ❖

Aristophanes the Mocker

THE COMING of the war had not interfered with the theater in Athens. Theatergoing, to an Athenian, was more than j... an amusement. It was a religious observance. Each year for more than a century now, plays had been presented at the Festival of Dionysus, and the people of Athens had voted on the best production.

Some of these plays were very solemn, especially those of old Aeschylus, who wrote lofty tragedies about gods and men. However, Aeschylus had died more than thirty years before, while visiting Sicily. The leading playwright at the moment was Sophocles, who was 70 years old but still busy with his pen. He had plays in competition just about every year, and he often won first prize. Another well-known author of tragedies was Euripides, who was fifteen years younger than Sophocles. Euripides also wrote many plays, but he rarely won the prize. His plays were too sophisticated, too unusual. He often seemed to be introducing strange new ideas that made Athens' theatergoers uneasy. Euripides was something of a troublemaker, and troublemakers are rarely popular. Quite likely he was a good friend of that other troublemaker, Socrates, though we have no proof of it.

Euripides was unpopular because he was using tragedy to criticize society. That was the wrong thing to do. Tragedy was supposed to be noble and uplifting, somber and grand. If a man wanted to poke fun at society, the Athenians felt, let him write comedy instead.

The comic plays that were performed each year at the Festival of Dionysus had developed later than tragedy. There had always been plenty of wild horseplay at the festivals, but the idea of giving that horseplay the shape of a play was still new, in the time of Socrates.

A young man named Aristophanes had set the new fashion. His plays lashed out at anything and everybody. Nothing was sacred to Aristophanes. He mocked all of Athens, and he was afraid of no one. Wherever he saw a weakness in Athenian society, he attacked it with all his might. He put real people in his plays, using their names and making them figures of fun. In 425, when he was only about twenty years old, Aristophanes had made the playwright Euripides a character in his play *The Acharnians*, and he had won first prize for comedy at the festival. A year later, he wrote *The Knights*, which made fun of Cleon, the most important political figure in Athens at the moment. Again, Aristophanes won the highest prize.

There was nothing subtle about the humor of Aristophanes. His jokes were broad and coarse, and the action of his plays often was pure slapstick. He did not mind being vulgar or even obscene to get a point across, and the people of Athens roared with laughter at lines that many of us would find shocking and distasteful. He did not try to be sly or witty; he went all out to jeer and mock, piling absurdity upon absurdity as he denounced rich men and poor men, wise men and stupid men, warmongers and peacemongers, statesmen and politicians. He was merciless in his mockery.

Now it was 423, and time for the festival. Aristophanes hoped to win first prize for the third year in a row. His new play was called *The Clouds*. Long before the festival, word began to circulate around Athens that his target for fun this time was the sophists. People smiled. Ah, yes, the foolish sophists, Aristophanes would make hash of them! But then came a new rumor. The special victim of the new play was going to be Socrates!

That seemed a little strange. Socrates, after all, was no sophist. He had done as much as any man in Athens to make the sophists look foolish, ever since his famous meeting with Protagoras, a dozen years before. And Socrates was known to be friendly with Aristophanes. Why should Aristophanes write a play mocking Socrates?

It was easy enough to see why, after a little thought. Socrates had become someone very important in Athens. He was the well-known seeker after truth, the man of many questions, a familiar public figure. That automatically made him a target for Aristophanes, to whom nothing was sacred. Besides, Socrates was so humorously ugly. Put an actor on stage made up to look like Socrates, with flat nose and big bulging eyes, and you were certain to reap a rich harvest of laughter. And maybe it was unfair to lump Socrates with the sophists, but what of that? Who said a comedy had to be fair?

Everyone in Athens looked forward to a treat at the

festival. Even Socrates, who probably knew he was going to be the butt of Aristophanes' humor, was eager to attend. He loved the fun of the festivals, and he had had to miss the plays last year, because he was away fighting at Delium. So certainly he was on hand to see *The Clouds*. Even if the joke were on him, he would not mind. He did not take himself so seriously that he could not laugh at his own expense.

There was no curtain, for the theater was simply an open-air auditorium with stone steps rising from a central stage. The actors appeared, and the thousands in the audience grew silent.

A character named Strepsiades came out. He was depicted as an old and stupid man from the countryside, who had moved to Athens and was trying hard to keep up with the high cost of living in the city. Strepsiades had one great problem: his son, Phidippides, who was an idle spendthrift. Phidippides was interested in nothing but the expensive sport of chariot-racing, which was the pastime of rich young men like Alcibiades. He had spent all of Strepsiades' money on chariots and horses and the expense of keeping a stable.

Strepsiades tells the audience that he has found a way to recover his fortune. Next door to Strepsiades' house is a place called the Thoughtery, where the sophists live and teach. Strepsiades will send his son to the Thoughtery. The sophists will teach the boy how to cheat and defraud. Strepsiades then will be able to outwit all the people he owes money to.

He wakes Phidippides up and says, "Do you see that little door and that little house?"

"Yes, father. But what are you driving at?"

"That is the Thoughtery of wise souls," Strepsiades says.

"There they prove that we are coals enclosed on all sides under a vast snuffer, which is the sky. If well paid, these men also teach one how to win lawsuits, whether they be just or not."

"What do they call themselves?"

"I do not know exactly, but they are deep thinkers and most admirable people."

Phidippides laughs. "Bah! the wretches! I know them; you mean those quacks with pale faces, those barefoot fellows, such as that miserable Socrates and Chaerephon?" He refuses to have anything to do with them. "What is it I should learn?" he asks.

"It seems they have two courses of reasoning, the true and the false, and that, thanks to the false, the worst lawsuits can be won. If then you learn this science, which is false, I shall not have to pay the debts I have contracted on your account."

Phidippides, though, will have none of it. He stalks away, saying that if, he spends any time in the Thoughtery, it would ruin his tan and leave him envious of the other horsemen.

Already, Aristophanes has been unfair to Socrates in many ways. He has said that Socrates teaches about the sky and the earth, which of course is untrue. He has twisted the idea of a Socratic dialogue into the "two courses of reasoning, the true and the false," claiming that Socrates teaches one how to make false reasoning win over true. And he has said that Socrates spends all his time indoors, whereas he was usually out in the market place or the gymnasium.

The fun was only beginning, though.

Strepsiades, unable to get his son to enroll as a pupil in the Thoughtery, decides to study there himself. He enters.

A disciple tells him that many important problems are
pondered there, such as the question, "How many times
the length of its legs does a flea jump?" They study astronomy, also, and geography, and many other things.

Then Strepsiades looks up and sees an odd sight: a man
suspended in a basket up in the middle of the air!

"Who is that?" he asks.

"That's *himself*," the disciple says.

"Who's himself?"

"Socrates."

"Socrates! Oh! I pray you, call him right loudly for me."

"Call him yourself," the disciple says. "I have no time to
waste."

Strepsiades calls out, and the basket swings toward him.
In a lofty voice, the actor pretending to be Socrates booms,
"Mortal, what do you want with me?"

"First, what are you doing up there? Tell me, I beseech
you."

Socrates explains: "I have to suspend my brain and
mingle the subtle essence of my mind with this air, which
is of the like nature, in order clearly to penetrate the
things of heaven. I should have discovered nothing, if I
had remained on the ground to consider from below the
things that are above; for the earth by its force attracts the
sap of the mind to itself. It's just the same with the water
cress."

In short: Socrates is a philosopher with both feet off the
ground.

Strepsiades begs to be admitted as a pupil. Socrates
grandly agrees to take him on. First, though, Strepsiades
must go through the rites of initiation. He must be presented to the Clouds, who are the greatest of goddesses.
Another jab at Socrates: Aristophanes is saying that Soc-

rates, unwilling to put up with Zeus and Athena and Apollo and the other gods, has invented some gods of his own, the Clouds.

With solemn mumbo jumbo, Socrates summons the Clouds. "They are great goddesses for the lazy," he tells Strepsiades. "To them we owe all, thoughts, speeches trickery, roguery, boasting, lies, sagacity. You never suspected they were goddesses, did you?"

"Oh, no, indeed," says Strepsiades. "I thought the Clouds were only fog, dew and vapor."

They are goddesses, Socrates repeats. Aristophanes gives him a really blasphemous line: "These are the only goddesses; all the rest are pure myth."

The Clouds speak. They hail Strepsiades, "who burns to instruct himself in fine language." And they greet Socrates, "great high priest of subtle nonsense," whom they obey because "you walk with head erect, a confident look, barefooted, resigned to everything and proud of our protection."

Strepsiades is troubled by all this. "Is our father Zeus not a god?" he asks.

"Zeus?" Socrates says. "What Zeus? Are you mad? There is no Zeus."

"But who causes the rain to fall?"

"The Clouds," Socrates says. "Have you ever seen it raining without clouds?"

"And who makes the thunder?"

"The Clouds, when they roll one over the other."

"But is it not Zeus who forces them to roll?"

"Not at all," Socrates replies. "It's the Whirlwind."

"Ah! I did not know that. So Zeus, it seems, has no existence, and it's the Whirlwind that reigns in his stead!"

Socrates now asks Strepsiades a few questions, to find out

what it is he wants to learn. The art of false reasoning, the old man replies. Socrates tries to instruct him, using a non-sensical imitation of the real Socrates' method of question-and-answer. Strepsiades, though, is too stupid to follow. The subtleties of Socrates bewilder him.

"Get out!" Socrates shouts. "You forget as fast as you learn!" He suggests that Strepsiades send his son Phidippides for instruction instead.

Strepsiades looks for Phidippides and shoves him violently in the general direction of the Thoughtery.

"By Zeus!" Phidippides cries, "you are no longer in your senses!"

"Oh, you fool! To believe in Zeus at your age!" Strepsiades says, laughing.

"Why do you laugh?" the puzzled Phidippides asks.

"Phidippides, there is no Zeus. The Whirlwind has driven out Zeus and is king now," the old man declares.

"What drivel!"

"You must realize that it is true."

"And who says so?"

"Socrates. And also Chaerephon, who knows how to measure the jump of a flea."

Phidippides thinks his father has gone mad. But, to humor him, he agrees to enroll at the Thoughtery. There, Phidippides is shown how to use false reasoning to triumph over truth—the method by which Ctesippus was taught that his father was a dog. Phidippides is a good pupil, and soon he graduates with all the skill of an accomplished sophist. Old Strepsiades is delighted. Now, he thinks, Phidippides will be able to argue his way out of all his debts, and go on to make himself a rich man through sophistry.

Soon, though, Strepsiades is less happy. He asks his son

to take his lyre and sing a song. Phidippides retorts that singing is a stupid thing to do. They quarrel, and Phidippides begins to beat his father.

"You villain!" Strepsiades cries. "Beating your own father!"

"Yes," says Phidippides. "And I will prove to you that I do right in beating you."

"Oh, wretch! Can it be right to beat a father?"

"I think I shall convince you so thoroughly that, when you have heard me, you will not have a word to say." And Phidippides explains: "Did you beat me in my childhood?"

"Why, certainly, for your good and in your own best interest."

"Tell me, is it not right, that in turn I should beat you for your good, since it is for a man's own best interest to be beaten? What! must your body be free of blows, and not mine? Am I not freeborn too? The children are to weep and the fathers go free?"

With elaborate sophistry, Phidippides "proves" that it is just and lawful to beat his own father—and his mother too. Strepsiades begins to see that he has made a mistake by filling his son's head with the dangerous ideas of Socrates.

"Show some reverence for Zeus!" he tells his son.

"There is no Zeus," replied Phidippides, parroting Strepsiades' own earlier talk.

Strepsiades turns to the statue of the god Hermes, and begs for forgiveness. "It was madness to let Socrates make me believe there were no gods," he moans. "What shall I do?"

Hermes offers a suggestion: burn down the Thoughtery. Strepsiades likes the idea. He calls to his friends. "Here, take a ladder, come forth and arm yourself with an axe.

Now mount upon the Thoughtery, demolish the roof! Ho, bring me a blazing torch! I will have vengeance!"

The building goes up in flames. A disciple appears and cries, "What are you doing?"

"I am entering upon a subtle argument with the beams of the house," answers Strepsiades.

Socrates comes to a window. "I am suffocating! I shall be burned up!"

"Ah! You insulted the gods! You studied the face of the moon!" Strepsiades shouts. As the sophists flee the Thoughtery, he runs after them, crying, "Chase them, strike them and beat them down! Forward! They have richly deserved their fate—above all, because of their blasphemies!" And the play ends in wild confusion, with the Thoughtery ablaze and the sophists taking to their heels.

The Athenians laughed merrily, but they did not vote Aristophanes first prize this time. He got third prize, which greatly disappointed him. Perhaps the other two plays were much funnier; we do not know, because their texts have not survived. Possibly the people were just tired of giving the prize to Aristophanes every year, or maybe they thought *The Clouds* did not measure up to his first two plays.

But we can be certain that nearly everybody was amused by the portrait of Socrates, unfair as it was. The ordinary spectator probably did not even know it was unfair. To him, Socrates was just another sophist, only uglier and more talkative than the rest. He was eccentric and often annoying, and that made him a good subject for comedy.

Yet the close friends of Socrates were probably upset by the cruel portrait. They knew that Socrates took no fees, gave no lectures, ran no school. He did not study matters of astronomy or geography, nor did he scoff at the gods. His friends did not see why Socrates should be held up to scorn and ridicule.

But Socrates did not complain. If Aristophanes wanted to have his little joke, so be it. Only a fool would try to defend himself against the barbs of Aristophanes, and Socrates was no fool. His friendship with the satirist does not seem to have been harmed. At least, they were together at the same banquet a few years later, apparently on good terms. Yet the mockery of *The Clouds* was destined to do Socrates great harm, many years afterward, at a time when Athenians were no longer able to distinguish between fantasy and reality.

8

❖ ❖ ❖

Of War and Philosophy

THERE WERE soon much more serious matters at hand than the mockery of Aristophanes. In April, 422, the one-year truce with Sparta ended. Cleon was now the most important man in Athens, and he was eager to renew the war. Certain that Sparta could be destroyed, he wanted to be the man who did it.

He talked the Athenian Assembly into making him a general and letting him go north to drive Brasidas out of the vital city of Amphipolis. The Assembly voted him a force of 1,200 hoplites, 300 cavalrymen, and 30 ships. Other cities of the League of Delos agreed to send soldiers to join the Athenians.

The expedition got under way at the end of August. One of the hoplites in Cleon's army was Socrates, who never shirked his duties as a soldier. Cleon succeeded in reconquering many of the towns that had fallen to Brasidas. Then, late in the season, he moved toward Amphipolis.

The allies that were supposed to help Athens retake Amphipolis had not yet arrived. But winter was coming on, some of Cleon's soldiers were impatient, and Cleon himself was hungry for glory. Without waiting for the allies, Cleon marched his men up to the stoutly defended walls of Amphipolis. Instead of digging in behind the walls, Brasidas ordered a surprise move: a sudden attack on the invaders. He led a Spartan army out of Amphipolis.

The Athenians, taken off guard, were thrown into confusion. They began to flee, though we can be sure Socrates stood his ground until the last moment. Cleon was one of those who ran, but the Spartans caught him and killed him. It was a jolting defeat for Athens.

Sparta, however, suffered an even greater loss. For in the moment of victory, Brasidas was struck down by an Athenian arrow. He was carried into Amphipolis, but died even as he learned that the Athenians were in flight. Sparta had lost her bravest and wisest general. In the three short years of his career, Brasidas had carried Sparta from the edge of defeat to the verge of victory.

The war had lasted ten years with but brief moments of truce. Both Athens and Sparta were tired of the destruction and the tragedy. And with Cleon and Brasidas gone, Athens and Sparta could think of peace.

Nicias, the new Athenian leader, negotiated a peace treaty in 421. Nicias, a speaker for peace, had been the political opponent of Cleon for many years. Now, this mild-mannered, extremely wealthy man won fame in Athens by bringing a halt to the war. The Peace of Nicias would last for 50 years, it was agreed. Amphipolis would be given back to Athens, along with certain other cities now held by

Sparta. All prisoners taken by both sides would be released. Athens agreed to let the cities of her League of Delos be self-governing, though they would continue to pay their contributions to Athens as before.

War-weary Hellas began to bind up her wounds. Socrates came home from the battlefield again and, since he was nearly fifty, was never to go to war again. He had seen action at Samos, at Potidaea, at Delium, at Amphipolis, and there was no one in Athens who could say he had not given generously of himself in defense of his city.

It was time for philosophy again. Socrates debated with everybody, but his questions stayed close to the same themes: What is courage? What is virtue? What is justice? In one discussion about courage, two important Athenians were there, Nicias, the peacemaker, and Laches, the general who had led the retreat from Delium. Laches was a good-natured man, not very bright but willing to learn, and he was glad to let Socrates quiz and query him.

"Tell me, if you can," Socrates asked, "what is courage."

"Easy," said Laches. "A man has courage if he does not run away, but stays at his post and fights against the enemy."

"Very well," said Socrates. "And I am sure, Laches, that you would consider courage to be a very noble quality."

"Most noble, certainly."

"And you would say that a wise endurance is also good and noble?"

"Very noble."

"But what would you say of a foolish endurance? Is that not on the other hand to be regarded as evil and hurtful?"

"True," said Laches.

"And is anything noble which is evil and hurtful?"

"I ought not to say that, Socrates."

"Then you would not admit that sort of endurance to be courage—for it is not noble, but courage is noble?"

"You are right."

"Then, according to you, only the wise endurance is courage?"

"True."

But what was "wise endurance"? Socrates next tried to find out. If a man stayed at his post because he knew the enemy was weak, was that courageous? It was certainly much more courageous, said Socrates, to remain at your post when you faced sure defeat. Laches admitted this.

"But surely, this is a foolish endurance in comparison with the other," Socrates said.

"That is true."

"And you would say that in a cavalry battle, he who is a good horseman and endures is not so courageous as the man who has no such skill and endures?"

"So I should say."

"And he who dives into a well, without any knowledge of diving, is more courageous than one who is a skilled diver and dives?"

"Why, Socrates, what else can a man say?"

"And yet men who run such risks and endure are foolish, Laches, in comparison to those who do the same things, having the skill to do them."

"That is true."

"But foolish boldness and endurance appeared before to be evil and hurtful to us."

"Quite true."

"Whereas courage was said to be a noble quality."

"True."

"And now, on the contrary, we are saying that the foolish endurance, which you agreed was dishonorable, is courage."

"Very true."

"And are we right in saying so? Can courage be foolish and hurtful and dishonorable?"

"Indeed, Socrates, I am sure that we are not right in saying that," Laches replied.

Socrates had led Laches into the same paradox with which he had snared Protagoras. How could courage be noble and foolish at the same time? Obviously something was wrong with Laches' idea of courage. With his line of questioning, Socrates had led Laches to stop and reexamine his basic thoughts about courage. The puzzled general said, "I fancy that I do know the nature of courage, only, somehow or other, she has slipped away from me, and I cannot get hold of her and tell her nature."

Then it was the turn of Nicias to try to succeed in defining courage where Laches had failed.

Socrates was always doing things like that: leading his friends into contradictions and paradoxes. He did not do it simply to amuse himself, but rather to open their eyes to the confusion of their thoughts. Long after Socrates was dead, even after Plato, clever men enjoyed writing dialogues in which Socrates appeared as a character who spun traps with words. Sometimes the Socrates of these later dialogues was every bit as wily and unfair as the sophists he condemned. He was shown proving all kinds of fanciful things through the use of Socratic questions. And these later dialogues sometimes led people to think that Socrates had been merely a clever word-juggler with nothing important to say.

For instance, in one such dialogue written several hundred years after the time of Socrates, he is shown debating the nature of true and false. He and a young man named Hippias are talking about the poems of Homer, and Hippias is arguing that Achilles, the bold soldier of *The Iliad,* was a man of truth, while clever Odysseus of *The Odyssey* was a false and tricky man.

Socrates gets Hippias to admit that the false, because they have the power to deceive, are powerful men. The false, they agree, must be very wise in order to be able to fool people.

"The false," asks Socrates, "are they those who are wise and have the power to speak falsely?"

Hippias agrees.

"Then a man who does not have the power of speaking falsely, and who is ignorant, cannot be false?" asks Socrates.

"You are right."

"And tell me, Hippias, are you not skilled in arithmetic?"

"Yes, Socrates, certainly I am."

"If someone were to ask you how much is three times seven hundred, you would tell him the true answer in a moment, if you cared to?"

"Certainly."

"Since you are the wisest and ablest of men in these matters, you are the most able to tell the truth about them, are you not?"

"That is right."

"And could you speak falsehoods about them equally well?" Socrates asks. He points out that Hippias could deliberately give the wrong answer, because he knows what the right answer is. But someone who is poor in arithmetic might not be able to tell a falsehood as easily. "Might he not sometimes stumble upon the truth, when he wanted to tell a lie, because he did not know, whereas you who are the wise man, if you wanted to tell a lie, would always and consistently lie?"

"Yes, there you are quite right."

"Then the same person is able to speak both falsely and truly about calculation? Who, then, Hippias, do we find to be false at calculation? Is he not the good man? For the good man is the able man, and he is the true man."

"That is evident."

"Do you not see, then, that the same man is false and also true about the same matters? I will remind you of what you were saying: were you not saying that Achilles was a true man, and Odysseus false and wily?"

"I was."

"And now do you see that the same person has turned out to be false as well as true? If Odysseus is false he is also true, and if Achilles is true he is also false, and so the two men are not opposed to one another, but they are alike."

"Oh, Socrates," cries Hippias, "you are always weaving the meshes of an argument, selecting the most difficult point, and fastening on details instead of grappling with the matter in hand as a whole! Everyone knows that Achilles is better and more truthful than Odysseus!"

He tries to prove what he says, but at once Socrates has him snared in worse confusion. Soon Socrates, still using his tricky methods, has forced Hippias into the strange paradox that a man who does evil by choice is better than a man who does evil involuntarily.

"There I cannot agree with you," Hippias says, after the argument has brought them to this impossible conclusion.

"Nor can I agree with myself, Hippias," Socrates says. "I find it quite perplexing. Now, it is not surprising that an ordinary man like me should be perplexed. But if you wise men, Hippias, are also puzzled, and we cannot come to you for aid, the matter begins to be serious both to us and to you." And there the discussion ends. Nothing has been proved, not much has been learned, but the Socrates of the dialogue has had some sophistic fun with poor Hippias.

Another time, Socrates had a more fruitful discussion, which Plato has recorded for us. It took place during the years of war, when plague was troubling Athens. A friend of Socrates, Theodorus by name, came to him to introduce an unusual young man named Theaetetus, a mathematician. "You must not be offended if I say that he is very like you," Theodorus told Socrates. "For he has a snub nose and projecting eyes, although these features are less marked in him than you. I never knew anyone who was his equal in natural gifts, for he has a quickness of mind which is almost unrivaled, and he is very gentle, and also the most courageous of men."

Socrates was pleased to meet the young mathematician. A "little difficulty" had recently been bothering him, he told Theaetetus. "I want you to aid me in investigating it. Will you answer a question for me: 'Is not learning growing wiser about that which you learn?' "

"Of course," said Theaetetus.

"And by wisdom the wise are wise?"

"Yes."

"And wisdom and knowledge, are they the same thing?"

"Yes," said Theaetetus.

"Here is the difficulty I can never solve to my satisfaction: What is knowledge? Can we answer that question?"

A discussion began. Instead of giving a general definition of knowledge, though, Theaetetus started by listing different kinds of knowledge: geometry, astronomy, harmony, and arithmetic, he suggested. Also the art of the shoemaker and the carpenter and the other craftsmen. "These, each and all of them, are knowledge."

"But that was not the point of my question," said Socrates. "We were not going to count the number of the arts and sciences. We wanted to know the nature of knowledge in general. Let me illustrate. Suppose a person were to ask about some very trivial and obvious thing. For example: What is clay? And we were to reply: there is a clay of potters, there is a clay of oven-makers, there is a clay of brick-makers. Would that answer not be ridiculous?"

"Truly."

"And when a man is asked what knowledge is, to give in answer the name of some art or science is ridiculous. For the question is, 'What is knowledge?' and he replies, 'A knowledge of this or that.' "

Theaetetus struggled but could not give Socrates a general definition of knowledge. It made him unhappy that he had failed to answer what seemed at first to be such a simple question. But Socrates reassured him. "You made a good beginning just now. Try and bring the many sorts of knowledge under one definition."

"I have tried, yet I cannot. Now I feel troubled and anxious."

"Those are the pangs of labor," Socrates said. "You have something within you which you are bringing to birth." And he added, "Have you never heard that I am the son of a midwife whose name was Phaenarete?"

"Yes, I have."

"And do you know that I am a midwife myself?"

"How can that be, Socrates?"

Socrates explained: a midwife, he said, was a woman who was past the age of having children, and who helped other women to give birth to theirs. Their task was a very important one. But Socrates had a task, too, even more important. He was a midwife of *ideas*.

"I look after the soul, not the body," he said. "Like the midwives, I am barren. The reproach which is often made against me, that I ask questions of others and have not the wit to answer them myself, is very just. The reason is, the gods compel me to be a midwife, but do not allow me to bring forth. And therefore I am not myself at all wise, nor have I anything to show which is the invention or birth of my own soul. Still, those who converse with me, profit."

He went on to say that he was different from real midwives in another way. For the children whom the midwives helped to bring into the world were always real children, while the ideas Socrates helped bring forth were sometimes true and noble, sometimes false. It was his task to tell whether an idea was true or false.

There were those, he said, who were angry when Socrates exposed one of their darling ideas as "a vain shadow." They were as angry as a woman whose child had been taken from her. "I have actually known some who were ready to bite me when I deprived them of a darling folly," said Socrates. "They did not realize that I acted from good will. I am not their enemy in all this, but it would be wrong for me to admit falsehood, or to stifle the truth. Once more, then, Theaetetus, I repeat my old question, 'What is knowledge?'—and do not say that you cannot tell, but acquit yourself like a man, and by the help of God you will be able to tell."

The questioning resumed. Soon the argument was raging thick and fast as Socrates drew ideas out of Theaetetus and helped him distinguish between true ideas and false ones. Theaetetus began to argue that knowledge was that which we can perceive with our senses. Borrowing an idea from Protagoras, he insisted that all our knowledge is derived from what we can see, hear, feel, smell or taste.

Socrates had some troublesome objections. What about the things we perceive in dreams? We certainly have false perceptions in our sleep. Are they part of our knowledge? No, Theaetetus said. They are only the phantoms of sleep.

"But how can you tell whether at this moment we are sleeping, and all our thoughts a dream, or whether we are awake and really talking to one another?" Socrates asked. "Perhaps this whole discussion is nothing but a dream of yours or mine."

Theaetetus was disturbed by that. Socrates next challenged the evidence of our senses. How can we trust our senses? When we are sick, wine may taste bitter to us, though it is sweet and pleasing when we are well. Is the wine bitter or sweet? Does that depend on whether we are sick or well? In that case, where is our knowledge?

And the same wine, he continued, might taste sweet to one person and bitter to another. The evidences of our senses, then, are not very reliable sources of knowledge. The theory must be discarded.

Theodorus, Socrates' friend, now broke in. "In heaven's name, Socrates, what *is* the truth?"

Socrates smiled. "You, Theodorus, are a lover of theories, and now you innocently fancy that I am a bag full of them, and can easily pull one out to take the place of the last one. But you do not see that really none of these theories come from me; they all come from him who talks with me."

So it was necessary to make a new start in the discussion. Before long, Theaetetus was at a standstill, and Socrates drew Theodorus into the debate. Onward and onward Socrates pursued the elusive definition of knowledge.

Theaetetus returned to the conversation, and gradually, with Socrates' help, worked his way to a new idea: that man perceived things, not only through his senses, but directly through his soul, or mind.

The new idea was this: that the eyes see various colors, but the mind sees the *idea of color*. The ear hears many sounds, but the mind perceives the *idea of sound*. So, too, does the mind perceive the ideas of warmth or cold, of softness or hardness, of bitterness or sweetness. Sometimes the senses of the body could give the wrong information, as when the body was ill. But the mind, with powers of its own, tried always to see the underlying ideas of all things.

Socrates replied, when Theaetetus said this, "You are a beauty, Theaetetus, and not ugly, as Theodorus was telling me. For he who utters the beautiful is himself beautiful and good. And besides being beautiful, you have done me a kindness in releasing me from a very long discussion, if you are clear that the soul views some things by herself and others through the bodily organs. For that was my own opinion, and I wanted you to agree with me."

Now Socrates moved toward an important conclusion. Knowledge was not simply the information received by the senses, as Theaetetus had tried to say before. "Knowledge does not consist in impressions of sense," said Socrates, "but in *reasoning about them*. In that only, and not in the mere sense impression, truth can be attained. Is this not so?"

"Assuredly," said Theaetetus.

The conversation was by no means over. Indeed, it continued for a long time afterward, as Socrates, eager to pursue this new idea he had helped Theaetetus bring forth, drew all the possible distinctions between knowledge and perception. There was much still to be examined, and many puzzling contradictions lay in store for them. They had to go on and ponder the causes of truth and error, the reasons why the senses did not always report the right information to the mind. They came to a new definition: "Knowledge is true opinion." It is, in other words, an insight into the nature of things, arrived at by reasoning and discussion.

But how did one know when an opinion was true? Ah, there was the stumbling block! And beyond that point Socrates could not go. They began to get into new difficulties at once, and so they had to halt. Socrates and Theaetetus had arrived at the realization that the more they talked, the more they discovered that real knowledge was impossible to attain. At least now they knew that they really knew nothing at all, and that understanding would make them better and humbler men.

9

❖ ❖ ❖

Shadows in the Cave

THE MOST FAMOUS of all the conversations of Socrates took place, so we think, during the year 421 B.C., the year the Peace of Nicias was signed. Our account of the things that were said comes from Plato, who was not present at the discussion. Perhaps Plato heard a summary of what had been said, or perhaps he invented the whole thing; we will never know. All that is certain is that about 380 B.C., long after Socrates was dead, Plato wrote a book called *The Republic,* which claimed to be an account of that celebrated conversation.

Even if Plato made up the whole story, we can still accept it as evidence of what Socrates was like and how he thought. Some of the political ideas expressed in *The Republic* are almost certainly Plato's, and not anything Socrates said. But the philosophical ideas are pure Socrates.

Sometime in 421 B.C., Plato tells us, Socrates went down

to the Piraeus, the port of Athens. The festival of the goddess Bendis was being held there, and Socrates went to
offer his prayers to her. Mostly, he was curious about the
festival. Bendis was a "new" goddess, from the northern
land of Thrace, and Socrates wanted to see what sort of
colorful procession would be staged to honor her, now that
her worship had reached Attica.

He was accompanied by Glaucon, the older brother of
Plato. They found the festival quite beautiful and spec-
tacular. As they prepared to leave for home, a man named
Polemarchus, son of the wealthy businessman Cephalus,
came running up to them. "Stay with us for supper,"
Polemarchus urged. "We have some interesting guests, and
tonight we can have a good talk."

Socrates and Glaucon went to the house of Cephalus.
They found a number of others there already, including a
famous sophist, Thrasymachus, from Chalcedon. Before
long, the assembled guests were deep in the Athenian's
favorite sport—serious conversation.

The topic was the nature of justice. Each guest in turn
tried to define what a just man was. One said that the just
man was one who spoke the truth and paid his debts. Another suggested that he was a man who did good to his
friends and did evil to his enemies. A third man offered
the opinion that a just man did good to his friends only
when his friends were good, and evil to his enemies only
when his enemies were evil. Socrates gently pointed out
the mistakes in these arguments with a few well-chosen
questions.

While this was going on, Thrasymachus was seething
with impatience. He kept trying to get a word in, but the
others would not let him interrupt. Finally, he lost his
temper. As Socrates told a friend the next day, "He came

at us like a wild beast, seeking to devour us. We were quite panic-stricken at the sight of him."

Thrasymachus roared, "What is wrong with all of you? Why do you sit around asking questions like this? Come right out, say what you mean!"

Socrates teased the sophist a little, in his usual fashion. "I am an ignorant man," he said, "and you are wise, Thrasymachus. Tell us about justice."

"What, and no payment!"

"I will pay when I have the money," Socrates replied.

But Glaucon said, "We'll all make a contribution for Socrates. Speak, Thrasymachus."

The sophist did not really expect to collect his usual fee for speaking. He merely grumbled, "Behold the wisdom of Socrates. He refuses to teach himself, and goes about learning of others, to whom he never even says thank you."

"I deny that," said Socrates. "I have no money, so I pay in praise, which is all I have. You soon will find out how ready I am to praise anyone who appears to me to speak well, for I expect that you will answer well."

Flattered, the sophist gave his definition: "Justice, I proclaim, is nothing else than the interest of the stronger. And now why do you not praise me? But, of course, you won't."

"Let me first understand you," said Socrates. "Justice, as you say, is the interest of the stronger. But what does this mean, Thrasymachus? You don't mean to say that because Polydamas, the wrestler, is stronger than we are, and finds the eating of beef good for him, that to eat beef is therefore equally good for us who are weaker than he is, and right and just for us?"

"That's abominable of you, Socrates," Thrasymachus retorted. "You take the words in the sense which is most damaging to the argument."

"Not at all, my good sir," Socrates said. "I'm trying to understand them. And I wish you would be a little clearer."

By skillful questioning, Socrates got Thrasymachus to expand on his idea. What the sophist was saying, simply, was that might made right. The stronger was just only because he was strong. It was the argument that many Athenians had put forth a few years before, at the time of the revolt of Mitylene. Was it just, men had asked, to massacre the people of Mitylene? "Yes," some had said. "It is just, because we are stronger than they are."

Socrates found this bloodthirsty doctrine not at all to his liking. He began to bait Thrasymachus, and before long had him thoroughly enmeshed in his own contradictions. The sophist grew angrier and angrier. He was certain he was right, but he could not defend himself against the gentle, insistent questions of Socrates.

At last he did what Protagoras had once done in a similar fix: he launched into a long-winded speech, hoping to silence Socrates that way. When he finished, he began to leave, but the company would not let him. "Stay and defend your position," they told him, and Socrates began to question him again.

He backed Thrasymachus neatly into a corner, until the sophist was forced to begin granting the points Socrates was making. "Then the just has turned out to be wise and good," Socrates said at last, "and the unjust evil and ignorant?"

"Yes, yes," Thrasymachus muttered, unhappily. It was a hot day and sweat was pouring from him in torrents. "And then I saw," reported Socrates later, "what I had never seen before, Thrasymachus blushing."

The hard-bitten sophist still refused to give in entirely.

"Don't suppose I approve of what you're saying," he told Socrates. "I'm still not convinced."

More questioning followed. Thrasymachus continued to retreat. At last, he admitted complete defeat. "Then the just man is happy, and the unjust man miserable?" Socrates asked.

"So be it."

"But happiness and not misery is profitable."

"Of course."

"Then, my blessed Thrasymachus, injustice can never be more profitable than justice."

Thrasymachus sighed and nodded. "Let this, Socrates, be your entertainment at the Festival of Bendis."

"For which I am indebted to you," Socrates said, "now that you have grown gentle toward me and left off scolding."

But Socrates went on to say that he had not really been well entertained, though it was his own fault. "I have gone from one subject to another without having discovered what I was really looking for—the nature of justice." Through the long conversation, they had discovered some things that justice was *not*, but not what true justice was. So the talk went on, far into the night, as the little group of friends began to help Socrates find out what justice was.

Socrates suggested that it might be easier to talk about justice in the polis, rather than justice in the individual man. A polis was bigger; if they could locate justice in the polis, they might be able to locate it in the individual.

For the rest of the night, Socrates and his friends spoke on the nature of the polis. Probably most of the thoughts were really Plato's, put for convenience and drama into the mouths of the guests at the home of Cephalus. Plato's book, *The Republic,* is the first book we know that tried to

imagine what an ideal community would be like, a community of justice and virtue. Today, we call such a community a "utopia," because that was the name of the ideal
state in a famous book by Sir Thomas More, written about
1516 A.D. Plato, almost 2,000 years earlier, wrote the first
of all utopian books.

Since we are not really concerned here with the ideas of
Plato, it is not necessary to look very deeply into the
thoughts expressed in the rest of *The Republic.* Much of
what Plato wrote stemmed from the ideas of Socrates, of
course, but a great deal more was Plato's contribution.

Sometimes we can clearly see which parts of the argument came from Socrates. For instance, a passage discussing the causes of war almost certainly sprang from the
mind of Socrates, that man of simple tastes and no luxuries.

A polis, Socrates declared, came into being because men
needed each other's skills. Farmers, builders, weavers, tool-
makers, merchants, sailors—all banded together to make
life better for everyone. At first, said Socrates, the polis was
concerned with basic things like raising food and building
houses for everyone. But then more complicated needs entered the picture:

"For I suspect that many will not be satisfied with the
simpler way of life. They will be for adding sofas, and
tables, and other furniture. They will want dainties, and
perfumes, and incense, and dancing girls, and cakes. The
arts of the painter and embroiderer will have to be set in
motion, and gold and ivory and all sorts of materials must
be obtained."

"True," said Glaucon.

"Then we must enlarge our borders, for the original
healthy polis is no longer sufficient." Slaves will be needed,

and musicians, poets, barbers, cooks, and many others who played no part in the original simple polis.

"And the country, which was enough to support the original inhabitants, will be too small now, and not enough?" asked Socrates.

"Quite true."

"Then a slice of our neighbors' land will be wanted by us for pasture, and they will want a slice of ours, if, like ourselves, they have given themselves up to the making of money."

"That, Socrates, will be inevitable."

"And so we shall go to war, Glaucon. Shall we not?"

"Most certainly," he replied.

Socrates was wise enough to realize that most men craved the luxuries he did without. So war, in the ordinary world, was sure to break out whenever human greed grew too strong. But what about the ideal polis? How can we depict a state where greed is unknown?

We can pass over Plato's discussion of the ideal polis because it probably has little connection with the thought of Socrates. But in the course of the long discussion, Plato makes Socrates say something that brilliantly illuminates the old philosopher's basic idea.

It is the same idea that we met in the conversation with Theaetetus. Then, Socrates was trying to get at the nature of knowledge. Theaetetus listed several different kinds of knowledge, but Socrates was looking for the idea of knowledge in general. In the debate with Protagoras, he was looking for the idea of virtue. In the conversation with Laches, Socrates was trying to find the idea of courage. Always an idea—always an abstract, invisible idea. Socrates did not want examples of courage or virtue or knowledge. He wanted the meaning of the ideas themselves.

And nowhere is this search for basic ideas put better than in *The Republic*. It was close to dawn before Socrates reached this point. All night the discussion had raged, and Socrates now was attempting to explain how difficult it is for men to reach the truth about any idea. At last, Socrates offered a vivid image to make his argument clear:

"Behold! Human beings living in an underground cave, which has a mouth open towards the light and reaching all along the cave. Here they have been since their childhood. Their legs and necks are chained so they cannot move. They can only see straight ahead of them because the chains prevent them from turning their heads around.

"Above and behind them is a fire blazing at a distance, and between the fire and the prisoners there is a raised way. And you will see, if you look, a low wall built along the way, like the screen which marionette players have in front of them, over which they show the puppets."

"I see," murmured Glaucon, contemplating the imaginary scene Socrates had conjured up.

"And do you see," Socrates went on, "men passing along the wall carrying all sorts of vessels, and statues and figures of animals made of wood and stone and various materials, which appear over the wall? Some of them are talking, others silent."

"You have shown me a strange image, and they are strange prisoners," said Glaucon.

"And the prisoners in the cave see only their own shadows, or the shadows of one another, which the fire throws on the opposite wall of the cave."

"True," said Glaucon, "for how could they see anything but the shadows if they were never allowed to move their heads?"

"And of the objects which are being carried along the way behind them, they would also see only the shadows?"

"Yes."

"And if they were able to talk with one another, would they not suppose that they were naming what was actually before them?"

"Very true."

"And suppose further that the prison had an echo which came from the other side, would they not be sure to think, when one of the passers-by spoke, that the voice which they heard came from the passing shadow?"

"No question," replied Glaucon.

"To them," Socrates said, "the truth would be literally nothing but the shadows of the images."

"That is certain."

Now, Socrates said, imagine that one of the prisoners were freed. Suddenly his bonds were removed, and he was allowed to stand up and turn around, and walk toward the light. "At first he will suffer sharp pains, and the glare will distress him. He will be unable to see the real objects of which, while a prisoner, he had seen only the shadows."

But then his vision would clear. Though dazzled by the light of the real world, he would gradually grow accustomed to it. The pain and irritation would pass away. He would be able to distinguish among shadows, and reflections in water, and real objects. "Then he will gaze upon the light of the moon and the stars and the spangled heaven. Last of all, he will be able to see the sun, and not mere reflections of him in the water."

He would come to realize, said Socrates, that the sun was the source of heat and light. And he would think of the cave, and the prisoners there, and how they had had to form all their ideas about the world simply on the basis of shadows against the cave wall. And he would pity them.

Suppose now, Socrates continued, that this man, after having had a glimpse of the sunlit world, were brought back into the darkness of the cave and chained once again. He would be unable to see in the cave until his eyes again became accustomed to darkness. The prisoners who had never left the cave would think him blind. "Men would say of him that up he went and down he came without his eyes, and that it was better not even to think of going up. And the prisoners in the cave would say that if anyone tried to free them and take them up to the light, they would refuse to go."

Now Socrates explained his strange parable of the cave:

The prison house is our ordinary world, and the fire in the cave is our sun. We see by that light, and what we see are really only shadows on a cave wall. For there is another world, a higher world. We cannot see it directly for we are as prisoners in a cave. We can only see flickering reflections, and make inaccurate guesses about the nature of that higher world.

Sometimes, Socrates said, a man is allowed to go up into the higher world and see reality as it actually exists. While he is there, he pities the poor prisoners in the cave. But when he comes back, he is dazzled by the light of the higher world, and returns groping and uncertain, to be laughed at by the prisoners of the shadow world.

And what is this upper world?

The world of ideas, Socrates said. The world of true forms.

He did not mean to say that such a place literally existed. He imagined it, merely as a convenient way to express his theory of ideas. The things of our world, said Socrates, are only shadowy images of ideal things.

For example: consider horses. There are many sorts of horses—young ones, old ones, black ones, red ones, stallions and mares, racehorses and workhorses, healthy horses and sick ones, small ones and big ones, slow ones and fast ones. What do they all have in common? They are all included in the *idea* of horses. Somewhere in this upper world of ideas, Socrates said, there is an "ideal horse," embodying all the qualities a horse can possibly have. The horses of our world all share, in some way, in the qualities of that ideal horse.

It is the same with everything else: that three-sided figure of geometry, the triangle, for instance. There are equilateral triangles and isosceles triangles and many other kinds of triangles. But they all have "triangleness." A figure is triangular so long as it has the necessary qualities of an ideal triangle—three sides, three angles adding up to 180°.

Chairs, tables, trees, fish, birds, houses, boats—all have their ideal forms, their patterns, their standard unit in the world of ideas. How do we explain what a tree is? Not by saying that it is oak, maple, pine or birch, but by relating it first to the *idea* of tree. Once we have established the "tree-ness" of an object, we can go on to describe it by saying what kind of tree it is.

And abstract ideas, of course, are found in that higher world—the idea of an idea, that is. The idea of knowledge is to be found there, embracing all the many kinds of knowledge, just as the idea of tree includes all the kinds of tree. Astronomy and geometry and carpentry and pot-making are all parts of the idea of knowledge, just as oak and pine and birch are parts of the idea of tree.

Plato used the word *eidē*, "form," to describe this theory. The plural of *eidē* is *ideai*, from which we get our word "idea." The Theory of Forms, or the Theory of Ideas, is really the work of Plato, but it had its roots in the teachings of Socrates. In his conversations Socrates always searched for the underlying forms, or ideas, of things. What is courage? What is virtue? What is knowledge? Socrates was trying to break his chains, get out of the cave, and see right into the world of ideas.

For, he said, ideas were eternal. A tree might wither, a horse might die, but the idea of the horse or the tree is perfect and everlasting. Our world, which is only the flickering shadow on the cave wall, can never attain the perfection of the ideal world. No line is ever perfectly straight in our world, no triangle is ever perfectly triangular. We can come close, but perfection is reserved for the ideal world alone.

Can we ever reach the ideal world? Can we free ourselves from the chains that hold us in bondage within the cave of our ignorance?

We can try, said Socrates. We can strive with all our hearts, and above all with all our minds, to break out of our prison. We can examine our thoughts, and struggle to understand the nature of reality, and work to ascend into that higher world of pure ideas. Perhaps that world could not be reached by mortal men; but, Socrates said, possibly after long struggle we might at least have a brief peep into that bright world of truth and perfection.

So the old flat-nosed philosopher said, as the first streaks of morning stained the gray sky over the house of Cephalus.

10

❖ ❖ ❖

A Banquet at Agathon's

An UNEASY PEACE had prevailed in Hellas since the treaty of Nicias in 421. But not everybody in Athens was happy with the terms of the truce. Sparta had laid down her arms, true, but some of Sparta's allies had never signed the treaty. Corinth, Megara, Boeotia, and other important enemies of Athens refused to make peace, although for the time being they stopped the actual fighting.

It was a peace that was not a peace. Athens could not be sure when the next attack might come. Many Athenians wished to cancel the treaty with Sparta. They knew that Sparta no longer wanted war, and they hoped to force her to bring her allies into line and sign a new treaty that would bring peace to all of Hellas.

One of the leaders of this anti-treaty group was Alcibiades. He was about thirty years old now. With Pericles dead, Alcibiades was moving into the position of leadership that had been predicted for him since boyhood. Not everyone trusted him, though. He was too hotheaded, too flashy. He drank too much. He had many followers in Athens, but could not get the kind of support that Athens had given Pericles.

Alcibiades had his own private ideas for insuring the safety of Athens. He did not like the idea of an alliance between Athens and Sparta, such as existed now. Sparta, he felt, could not be relied upon. So he went off to the city of Argos to stir up some trouble.

Argos was one of the oldest cities of Greece. She had been great and powerful hundreds of years before, when Athens and Sparta had been nothing but muddy villages. Argos was a city of the Peloponnesus, the region of Greece where Sparta was, but the Argives had refused to let themselves be drawn into a conflict with their warlike neighbor. During the ten years of war between Athens and Sparta, Argos had gone her own way and grown prosperous, unharmed by war.

Alcibiades tried to talk the Argives into an Argos-Athens alliance against Sparta. The wary Argives were easy prey for Alcibiades' glamour and glibness, and an alliance was formed. At home, Nicias objected, but the followers of Alcibiades had their way. In 419, Alcibiades was elected general, with a rank equal to that of Nicias.

Sparta, naturally, was unhappy to see Athens allying herself with powerful Argos. When Argos, bolstered by her treaty with Athens, began to invade neighboring towns, the Spartans took action. They sent an army toward Argos.

Athens was bound by the new treaty to defend Argos. Southward went General Alcibiades, with 1,000 hoplites, in 418. It seemed as if Athens and Sparta would once again be at war. Wiser heads won out this time; the Spartans backed away from Argos, and there was no battle. In Athens, Nicias called Alcibiades a dangerous warmonger who had nearly caused the end of the peace. The next year, Alcibiades was not re-elected general.

Argos now realized that Alcibiades did not speak for all of Athens. "This man nearly got us into war with Sparta," the Argives said. "He promised Athens would defend us if Sparta attacked. But what is his promise worth? We are better off remaining friendly with Sparta."

The Athens-Argos alliance broke up. Argos now allied herself with Sparta. The political situation grew enormously complicated, with alliances coming and going every month. An ominous tension developed. There had been no war for five years, but trouble was soon to start. Alcibiades, impetuous and bold, the darling of Athens, grew more popular. Nicias, the mild-mannered peacemaker, lost influence. Alcibiades was elected general once again. He gloried in his renewed importance.

Athens, carried away by headstrong Alcibiades, began to look around for places to test her strength. The year was 416. Alcibiades had shown his personal grandeur by entering no less than seven four-horse teams in the chariot race of that year's Olympics. He broke all records; his chariots finished first, second, third, and fourth! He moved with lordly dignity now, acclaimed by all. Even the playwright Euripides, usually aloof from such things, was coaxed into writing an ode of victory to Alcibiades when he returned from the Olympics with news of his great triumph.

Athens and Alcibiades wanted new triumphs now.

One stubborn little city had been annoying them. This was Melos, once a Spartan colony. The other cities on the island where Melos was located had been conquered by

Athens in 426, but the city of Melos alone had held out. Now, in 416, Athens sent a fleet of 38 ships, with 3,420 troops, to deal with Melos.

The Athenian general ordered the Melians to surrender their city and pay tribute to Athens.

"Why should we?" the rulers of Melos asked. "We are neutral and independent. We want nothing to do with Athens. Why must we pay tribute to you? Is this what you Athenians call justice?"

The Athenians' answer was blunt and straightforward. They wanted tribute, not because Athens had overthrown the Persians, and not because Melos had done Athens any wrong, and not because Melos had once been a Spartan colony, but simply because Athens was stronger than Melos. "We will use no fancy language with you," the Athenians told the Melians. "You know as well as we do that the powerful take what they can get, and the weak yield what they must."

The Melians were horrified by this cold-blooded approach. Would Pericles ever have said such a thing? What had happened to wise, tolerant Athens?

"Submit," the Athenians insisted. "Otherwise you will meet a terrible fate."

"Let us remain neutral," the Melians begged. "We will stay at peace, friendly toward Athens instead of being your enemy, taking no part in the war."

"No. If we let you stay neutral, it would be a sign of our weakness. If you came to hate us, it would be a proof of our power."

It was the voice of Thrasymachus speaking, arguing that might made right. But this was no mere philosophical debate. The fate of an independent city was at stake. The

Athenians withdrew, advising the Melians to think it over: submit or perish, and no talk of justice.

The Melians decided to resist. Athenian soldiers lay siege to the city, and conquered it after many months. All the grown men were slaughtered. The women and children were sold into slavery. Might had triumphed. The massacre at Melos was the clearest sign of what had happened to Athens. The city had lost its old nobility, had become cruel and vengeful. In 427, Athens had drawn back at the last moment from destroying Mitylene this way; but in 416 there was no mercy for hapless Melos.

And Alcibiades found a new chance for Athens to flourish her military might.

The island of Sicily, off the tip of Italy, had been peopled by colonists from Greece. Some of the cities of Sicily had grown to great size. The most powerful of all was Syracuse, a colony founded by Corinth. Syracuse had swallowed up several neighboring Sicilian cities. Now she was making menacing gestures toward the city of Segesta, an ally of Athens.

Alcibiades urged a military expedition against Sicily. He wanted to smash Syracuse before she grew even stronger. By gaining control of Sicily, Athens would also cut off a trade route through which Sparta and the other Peloponnesian cities got grain from Syracuse.

Alcibiades persuaded the Athenian Assembly to vote an expedition of 60 warships. The purpose of the expedition would be to defend Segesta; to free Leontini, another Athenian ally that had already been conquered by Syracuse; and "to settle all other matters in Sicily as they might deem best for the Athenians." Alcibiades, of course, was named as one of the generals to lead this mighty expedition. But the Athenians still did not fully trust the dashing

Alcibiades. To keep watch over him, they named two other generals. One was Lamachus, a good soldier who had no political following. The other was Alcibiades' rival, Nicias, who did not want war at all.

Nicias opposed the whole idea of the expedition to Sicily. But, since the Assembly had voted it, he agreed to go. That way, at least, he could keep Alcibiades from running wild in Sicily and perhaps touching off full-scale war once again.

While this vast armada was being assembled, the Athenians went about their city life as usual. The Festival of Dionysus was held, plays were presented, and a rich man named Agathon, who had a leaning toward the arts, won first prize for a tragedy he had written. Agathon gave a banquet to celebrate his victory, and among those invited was Socrates.

The invitation actually was for a *symposium*, which originally meant "a drinking together." Today, we use the word "symposium" to mean a formal discussion, But the Greeks had a different understanding of the word.

A symposium followed a banquet. The guests ate on couches, reclining and supporting themselves on their left elbows as they ate. (Only women ever sat in chairs when eating, and women were not invited to such parties.) When the dinner dishes were cleared away, the symposium proper began. The guests would elect a "president," or toastmaster, who would govern the drinking. He decided how much water was to be mixed with the strong Greek wine, and how much wine there would be in each glass. At least, he did so at the beginning of the symposium. Later on, when everyone had had plenty of wine, the formal regulations were usually forgotten.

There customarily was professional entertainment at a

symposium, supplied by musicians and dancers. Then the guests would talk, each in turn perhaps making a speech on some topic that all had agreed upon. Even when they relaxed, the Athenians believed in keeping their minds busy. Their highest form of relaxation, in fact, was a good debate accompanied by plenty of good wine.

Socrates set out for Agathon's house early in the evening. He had gone first to the public baths, and then, on the way to Agathon's, he met a friend, Aristodemus. Aristodemus was startled to see that Socrates was wearing shoes, something most unusual for him.

"Where are you going in all that finery?" Aristodemus asked.

"To dinner with Agathon," Socrates said. "One must look one's best when one is going to visit such a fine man. What do you say to coming with me?"

"But I haven't been invited!"

"That doesn't matter," said Socrates. And he quoted a line from Homer to prove that it was no crime to go unasked to a great man's banquet. So off they went together, but soon Socrates became lost in thought, and began to walk more slowly. Aristodemus waited for him.

"Go on ahead without me," said Socrates.

Aristodemus reached Agathon's house. He was in an odd position, though, since he was not invited, and Socrates, who had invited him to come along, was nowhere in sight. Agathon made him welcome, however.

"I'm glad you came," he told Aristodemus. "I tried to find you yesterday to invite you, but you weren't anywhere to be found. Why haven't you brought Socrates with you, though?"

"I was with him until a moment ago," said Aristodemus.

"It was Socrates who invited me, as a matter of fact. But I can't think what has become of him."

Agathon sent a servant to look for Socrates, while Aristodemus entered the party. Aristophanes was there, the jeering comic playwright who had made such merciless fun of Socrates in *The Clouds* seven or eight years before. A doctor named Eryximachus was another guest, and Phaedrus, a poet, and Pausanias, a friend of Agathon. They were all sprawled out on their couches, waiting for dinner to begin.

The servant who had gone to look for Socrates returned. Socrates, he reported, was standing on the front porch of a neighboring house, deep in thought. He had not seemed to listen when the servant asked him to go to Agathon's.

"What an odd thing," said Agathon. "Go and call him again, and don't take 'no' for an answer."

"No, let him alone," said Aristodemus. "It's a way he has. He goes off sometimes and stands still wherever he happens to be. He'll come along, sooner or later."

Agathon shrugged, and ordered the servants to begin serving dinner. Socrates finally arrived when dinner was half over.

"Come sit next to me," Agathon called. "Perhaps the discovery you just made on the porch will flow into me, and I'll become wiser."

Socrates sat down, saying, "It would be very nice, Agathon, if wisdom flowed like water out of a person who has more into a person who has less. In that case, I'll be glad to sit beside you, for you have much wisdom and I have little."

When dinner was over and the drinking was about to begin, Pausanias suggested that they take it easy tonight, for they had all done plenty of drinking the night before.

The doctor, Eryximachus, agreed. "My medical experience has convinced me that drunkenness is bad for people," he said solemnly. So it was agreed that there would be no heavy drinking or boisterous behavior at tonight's symposium. And the musicians and dancers would be sent away. Instead, the guests would hold a serious discussion on some philosophical topic, each in turn making a speech. The topic chosen was the nature of love.

Phaedrus spoke first. As a poet, he spoke in flowery terms, praising love because it instils a sense of honor and self-sacrifice in men. Then Pausanias spoke, saying not very much in a great many words. It was the turn of Aristophanes next, but the comic poet had developed a case of hiccups. He turned to his neighbor, Eryximachus, and said, "You speak in my place, and perhaps the hiccups will stop."

Dr. Eryximachus rose to speak. First he offered a prescription for Aristophanes' hiccups: "Hold your breath for a good time while I'm speaking. If that doesn't work, gargle with water, or get something to tickle your nose with, and sneeze. The sneezing will stop your hiccups."

Having dispensed this medical advice, Eryximachus gave a "scientific" explanation of the mysterious phenomenon known as love. Then Aristophanes, his hiccups cured, made a playful and fantastic speech, full of fun, in which he said that long ago there had been neither men nor women, but only strange creatures with two faces, four arms, and four legs. Zeus had sliced these beings in half. Love, said Aristophanes, was simply the yearning of every half-creature to be reunited with his other half.

It was an amusing and poetic idea, and Aristophanes was praised highly when he finished. Then came the turn of Agathon, the host, who was very conscious that he had to

live up to his new reputation as a prize-winning playwright. He gave a high-flown and literary speech, full of
elegant phrases, and drew loud applause from his friends.

Everyone had spoken except Aristodemus, who did not
plan to speak, and Socrates. "I am at a loss for words,"
Socrates said. "I could never hope to match the eloquence
of Agathon. I can't equal any of you. I won't make a
speech for I'd only be a laughingstock if I tried to compete
with you." He said that he would make a plain statement
of what he thought was the truth about love. The others
encouraged him to speak in any way he saw fit.

He began in his familiar fashion by asking questions. He
quizzed Agathon about the nature of love, and soon got
the playwright to agree that love was a want, a need, a lack.
Love was a yearning after something, Socrates showed. But
a yearning after what?

Instead of delivering a direct lecture on his ideas, which
would have been out of character for him, Socrates related
the story of his meeting with a wise woman, Diotima of
Mantinea. Years ago, he said, he had discussed the nature
of love with her, and she had told him many things he had
not known before.

There were many different kinds of love, Diotima told
Socrates: not only the love of a beautiful man or woman,
but also the love of wisdom, the love of the laws, the love
of science. She explained that there was a "ladder of love,"
which every intelligent person should attempt to climb.

First, when a man was young, he should contemplate
physical beauty. He should fall in love with one particular
beautiful person. But soon, if he had wisdom, he would
come to see that there were many beautiful people in the
world, not just one. Instead of loving one person only,
he would love all beautiful forms.

"The next stage," according to Diotima, "is for him to value beauty of soul more than beauty of body." Outward appearance would no longer matter. What he would love, now, would be the virtuous soul. The love of inner beauty would lead him to a love for laws and institutions of mankind, which are beautiful because they preserve order and peace. "Here, too, he will recognize that all beauty is akin. He must look next at the beauty of the sciences. By gazing at the vast ocean of beauty to which his attention is now turned, he may bring forth from his love of wisdom many beautiful and magnificent sentiments and ideas."

And then, at last, he would reach the top of the ladder of love. No longer would he be concerned simply with the beauty of the body, or of the soul, or of the laws, or of the sciences. He will come to behold pure beauty itself, the *idea* of beauty. He will have entered that world of ideas, that higher world, to which our world is just a pattern of wavering shadows on the wall of a cave.

"He will suddenly have revealed to him," Diotima had told Socrates, "a beauty whose nature is marvelous indeed, the final goal, Socrates, of all his previous efforts. This beauty is, first of all, eternal. It neither comes into being nor passes away. It is not beautiful in part and ugly in part, nor beautiful at one time nor ugly at another. It is not a beauty that depends on the beholder. It is absolute, existing alone with itself, unique, eternal. All other beautiful things partake of it."

So love, for Diotima—and for Socrates—was a means of ascending into this realm of pure ideas. Climbing the ladder of love, one can at last enter the higher world.

"This above all others, my dear Socrates," Diotima concluded, "is the region where a man's life should be spent, in the contemplation of absolute beauty. Once you have seen that, you will esteem it far beyond gold and rich garments and the beauty of the body. How happy is the man who sees absolute beauty, pure and unalloyed! Do you think that it will be a poor life that a man leads who has his gaze fixed in that direction? He who can see true beauty can bring forth true goodness, not just reflected images of goodness. And having brought forth and nurtured true goodness, he will have the privilege of being beloved of God, and becoming, if ever a man can, immortal himself."

That was what Diotima had told Socrates; and that, Socrates declared, was what he himself now believed. And so he went about Athens, trying to help people see into the world of ideas, and himself trying to penetrate that realm of pure beauty.

His speech was over. He had said a great deal, and the guests, as they applauded him, must have been in a suddenly sober and thoughtful mood as they considered the thoughts of Socrates. But the philosophical mood was shattered a moment later. There came a loud knocking at the door. It sounded like a party of carousers outside, and the music of flutes could be heard.

A moment later, the banqueters heard the voice of Alcibiades in the courtyard. He was very drunk, and kept shouting, "Where is Agathon? Take me to Agathon!"

Then he came lurching into the banquet hall, wobbling a little. He was crowned by a wreath of ivy and violets, and he leaned against a companion. "Hail, friends!" he cried. "Will you welcome into your company a man who is already drunk, very drunk, or shall I just put a garland on Agathon, which is what I came for, and go away?" He had come to crown Agathon with a wreath, in honor of his victory in the tragedy contest. "Can I join your party? Will you drink with me or not?"

Everyone loudly called for him to join in. His wreath was over his eyes, so he could hardly see. He dropped down on the couch next to Agathon. Socrates moved over to make room for him. Pushing the wreath out of the way, Alcibiades turned and saw Socrates beside him.

"Pardon me, Agathon," Alcibiades said. "I must crown Socrates with this wreath as well as you. I could not leave him uncrowned for his words bring him victory over all men at all times, not just on one occasion, like yours the day before yesterday." He divided the wreath in two, and crowned both Agathon and Socrates.

Then Alcibiades looked around. "Come, sirs, you all seem quite sober. This can't be allowed! Bring a cup of wine, Agathon—a big cup!" A slave brought wine, and Alcibiades drank deeply. "Fill it again," he said, "and let Socrates drink, too. Not that it will have any effect on him. He can drink any quantity at all, and never be drunk."

Then Eryximachus said, "Tonight we are not simply drinking, Alcibiades, but are amusing ourselves in conversation." He explained how each man present had made a speech in praise of love. It was now the turn of Alcibiades, Eryximachus said.

"An excellent idea, Eryximachus," replied Alcibiades. "But it can't be fair to make a man who's drunk compete in speaking with men who are sober." The man who would soon be general of the expedition to Syracuse roared with laughter and announced that he refused to praise love, anyway. He would praise Socrates, instead.

"What are you doing?" said Socrates. "Are you going to raise a laugh at my expense? Or what?"

"I am only going to speak the truth, if you'll allow it."

"Of course I allow the truth," said Socrates. "I even invite you to speak, if you'll speak truth."

With many a drunken bow, Alcibiades commenced his speech in praise of Socrates. He began by comparing him to the ugly little statuettes of Silenus sold in Athenian shops, for was not Socrates as ugly as Silenus? He compared him, too, to Marsyas, the mythological flute player. But Socrates was greater than Marsyas for Marsyas had needed an instrument in order to charm men, while Socrates could cast a spell over everyone with mere words.

"But when he tries to speak to me, I stop up my ears and flee," said Alcibiades. "For he makes me confess that I should not live the way I do, busying myself with politics instead of tending to the needs of my soul. He is the only person who ever made me ashamed—yes, even I can feel shame!—for I know that I can't answer him or say that I should not do as he bids. But when I leave him, the love of popularity gets the better of me. So I behave like a runaway slave and take to my heels, and the next time I see him, I feel ashamed. Many a time I've wished that he would vanish from the face of the earth, but I know that if it happened, I'd be much more sorry than glad. In fact, I'm at my wit's end about Socrates."

Then he spoke of the way Socrates liked to pretend he was an ignorant man. It is only a mask, Alcibiades said. "He spends his whole life pretending and playing with people, and I doubt whether anyone has ever seen the treasures which are revealed when he grows serious and exposes what he keeps inside. But within him are divine and precious and beautiful and marvelous things."

Alcibiades talked next of Socrates' indifference to comfort and danger. He remembered the way Socrates had marched barefoot over the ice at Potidaea, and how he had stood in one spot all day while working out some difficult problem. He spoke of the bravery of Socrates at the retreat from Delium.

In closing, Alcibiades said, "The really wonderful thing about Socrates is that he is like no other human being, living or dead." Such men as Brasidas or Pericles could be compared to heroes out of Homer. But there had never been anyone remotely resembling Socrates. He was unique.

"Anyone who sets out to listen to Socrates talking will probably find his conversation utterly ridiculous at first, it being clothed in such curious words and phrases. He talks of pack-asses and blacksmiths, cobblers and tanners. He seems to express the same ideas in the same language over and over again, so that any ordinary person is bound to laugh at him. But if a man penetrates within, and sees what Socrates is really saying, he will find that there is nothing but sound sense there, that this talk is almost the talk of a god."

Alcibiades had finished his praise of Socrates. There was laughter and applause. The banqueters joked with one another for a while. Then a crowd of revelers, coming from some other party, wandered by. They found the door to Agathon's house open, and came right into the dining room. There was a general uproar and all discussion ended. Some of the guests, such as Phaedrus and Eryximachus, went home. Others joined in the wild drinking.

All this time, Aristodemus, the friend of Socrates who had come uninvited to the symposium, had been sitting quietly, taking everything in without saying anything. Now Aristodemus fell asleep. The crowing of the roosters woke him in the morning. He saw that nearly everyone had left or had dropped off to sleep. Only Socrates, Agathon, and Aristophanes were still awake.

They were having a discussion. Socrates was doing practically all the talking, and the other two, sleepy and woozy from wine, were trying to follow his arguments. The subject was poetry, and Socrates was insisting that any man who could write a comedy could also write a tragedy. A true artist should be able to turn his hand to either form, argued Socrates.

Before long, Aristophanes began to nod and then to doze. A little while later, Agathon was snoozing, too, just as the day dawned. Socrates, having put both of his friends to sleep, rose and went away, followed by Aristodemus. Although he had been up all night, drinking and speaking, Socrates was still wide awake. He went to the gymnasium and took a bath, and then passed the day as he would any other, debating with the men he met at the gymnasium. When evening came, he went home to bed, and no doubt he slept quite soundly.

11

❖ ❖ ❖

Athens in Torment

As THE TIME for the departure of the expedition drew
near, a kind of hysterical gaiety held sway in Athens. The
citizens were giddy with excitement. Night after night,
bands of revelers roamed through the city, making merry.
There was a feeling that great triumph lay just ahead.
How could so grand a fleet fail to win victory? Sicily would
fall to Athens. Athens would become so powerful that no
other polis of Greece would dare to oppose her. The con-
quest of Sicily would make every Athenian a rich man,
some said. Tribute would flow like a river into the treasury
of Athens.

Suddenly the hysteria turned into panic. On a night in
June, 415, a band of merrymakers committed an act of
sacrilege. Every temple and private home had a statue in
its doorway, called a *herma*—a block of stone, with the face
of the god Hermes at its top. On this night, most of the

hermae of Athens were battered and mutilated. It was an evil omen for the great expedition.

Worse, people began to whisper that General Alcibiades himself was responsible! Soon everyone was saying it. While drunk, it was said, Alcibiades and some of his wild young friends had gone on a herma-smashing rampage.

He denied any part in the scandal. There was talk of bringing him to trial but the expedition was about to leave for Sicily. Ships from Argos and Mantinea had joined the armada, and it was feared that these allies would withdraw if Alcibiades lost his command position. So the expedition sailed on time. It was the costliest and most splendid fleet that any Greek city had ever sent to sea.

The three generals, Alcibiades, Nicias, and Lamachus, could not agree on strategy once they had reached Sicily. Nicias wanted to help the city of Segesta maintain its freedom from Sicily, and then depart. Alcibiades argued that they should build up an alliance of many cities and attack Syracuse. Lamachus, the best soldier of the three, pointed out that Syracuse was still unprepared for an attack. If they struck right away, Syracuse would fall without a struggle. There was no sense giving Syracuse time to arm, Lamachus said.

While the generals quarreled, there was trouble on the home front. Athens was seething with rumors. One story had it that a small group of aristocrats was going to overthrow the democratic government of Athens and establish a tyranny. The mutilation of the hermae had been the first move of the subversives, it was said. And Alcibiades, so the rumor insisted, was the leader of this anti-democratic underground.

There were arrests and some executions. The Assembly voted to bring Alcibiades home from Sicily and put him on trial. An official city ship was sent to fetch him. When he heard what was going on, Alcibiades slipped away and disappeared—heading for Sparta!

That seemed clear proof of the guilt of Alcibiades. So the Athenian Assembly voted a death sentence against him in his absence. All his popularity, all his brilliance mattered not at all. In only a few months, Alcibiades had gone from honored general to hunted outlaw.

In Sicily, Nicias and Lamachus continued to quarrel over the strategy of the expedition. Finally Nicias attacked the Syracusan army and won a notable victory. But instead of following up his triumph by an invasion of the city, he held back. Syracuse rebuilt her defenses. She sent messengers to Corinth and Sparta, asking for help. Corinth agreed at once to aid Syracuse against the Athenian foes. But would Sparta, still officially at peace with Athens, enter the conflict?

Alcibiades was in Sparta now. An exile from Athens, he had taken refuge with the greatest enemy Athens had. "True," he told the Spartans, "I have injured Sparta in the past. But see how Athens has injured me! I come to join you."

Alcibiades urged Sparta to go to the aid of Syracuse. If Sparta did not, he said, all Sicily would fall to Athens, and Sparta would be in grave danger. But the Spartans did not immediately supply troops. They merely loaned Syracuse a general, Gylippus, to take charge of her army.

Under Gylippus, the Syracusans surrounded the Athenian force and cut it off. Nicias sent a message home, asking for more money, more ships, more soldiers—and for a new general because he was seriously ill and wanted to return to Athens. The Athenian Assembly sent reinforcements to

Nicias, and two new generals, Demosthenes and Eurymedon. But Nicias was ordered to remain in Sicily.

Alcibiades went on stirring up trouble in Sparta. He
persuaded the Spartans to renew the war against Athens.
He coaxed them into sending 1,600 soldiers to Gylippus,
and at the same time got them to invade Attica once again.
Soon the Spartans had taken possession of Decelea, a town
only 14 miles from Athens, and had built a fort there. Off
in Sicily, the troubled Athenian expedition was under attack from many sides. The high hopes of 415 B.C. had
turned into despair for Athens.

The reinforcements under Demosthenes arrived in Sicily. But the Athenians' first attack on Syracuse was hurled
back. Demosthenes began to talk of pulling out of Sicily
and going home to defend Athens. Nicias argued that they
should remain and fight. He did not want to face the
Athenian Assembly again without having conquered Syracuse.

The Athenians lost battle after battle. Eurymedon, one
of the generals, was killed. The entire Athenian fleet made
one last great attempt to enter the harbor of Syracuse, but
the stubborn Syracusans held firm. Dozens of Athenian
warships were burned. The soldiers panicked and a terrible retreat began. Ships and soldiers of Syracuse blocked
the surviving Athenians wherever they turned. Demosthenes and 6,000 men surrendered. Nicias and his men
pushed on until they came to a river blocked by soldiers
from Syracuse. After a horrifying massacre of Athenians,
Nicias too surrendered.

The great expedition had met with utter destruction.
Nicias and Demosthenes were put to death by the Syracusans. Lamachus, the third of the three original generals,
was luckier: he had died a hero's death in battle. Thou-

sands of Athenian soldiers became slaves. Hundreds of Athenian ships had gone to the bottom of the sea. It was a catastrophe so enormous that at first Athens could not believe it. Everyone lost? All the ships sunk? Impossible!

There was a great stirring among the subject cities of Athens' empire. There was much talk of revolt now. Some neutral cities considered allying themselves with Sparta to wipe out proud Athens for good and all.

Athens was in confusion and torment. People milled helplessly in the streets. With the great armada destroyed, and Spartan armies only a few miles from the city, what would become of Athens? Disaster seemed certain.

Revolution feeds on panic. A group of army officers seized control in Athens. They set up an emergency committee, the Committee of Four Hundred, to rule the city. The supporters of Athenian democracy fled to the city of Samos. The exiles in Samos declared that they were the true Athenians, not the Four Hundred who had grabbed power. They sent word to Alcibiades, inviting him to come home and help them expel the Four Hundred.

Why Alcibiades, of all people? Because he had made another switch of loyalty. He had left Sparta and struck up a friendship with an important Persian named Tissaphernes. Astonishingly, Alcibiades had dared to negotiate a new alliance—with Persia! "Sparta is your real enemy," he told the Persians. "Help Athens defeat Sparta, and it will be a good thing both for Athens and for Sparta."

Alcibiades desperately wanted Athens to forgive him and call him home. He felt that the only way he could achieve this was to have something to offer that Athens needed. He did: the promise of Persian support. In her time of need, then, Athens turned to Alcibiades—who had already deserted her once for Sparta—and to Persia, which once had been the enemy of enemies. In wartime, old grievances are quickly forgotten when danger is at hand.

Alcibiades went to Samos and was hailed by the exiles as a savior. The democratic exiles gathered their strength and prepared to invade Athens. The Four Hundred, meanwhile, were in a shaky position. They had little popular support among the Athenians, and they were trying without luck to make peace with Sparta. In 411, the Four Hundred were overthrown. The Athenian Assembly regained power and invited the exiles to return.

Alcibiades was back in command.

The Persians never did enter the war directly. Under Alcibiades, the Athenians scored some important naval victories against the Spartans. In 407, as a conquering hero, he returned to Athens. He addressed the Assembly, denied all the charges that had been made against him, and vowed his loyalty to the polis. The Athenians acclaimed him wildly, and gave him complete charge of the war with Sparta.

His moment of glory was brief. The Spartans had an able new general, Lysander. Alcibiades was wary of Lysander, knowing what a good soldier he was, and avoided meeting him in battle. But toward the end of the year 407, Alcibiades temporarily put the Athenian fleet in the command of a friend of his named Antilochus. Antilochus rashly attacked Lysander's fleet, and suffered heavy losses. The Athenian Assembly, forever changing its mind about Alcibiades, removed him from his position of command. Sulking, he withdrew to his castle.

The war seesawed wildly. In 406, the Athenian fleet met the Spartans near the Arginusae, a small group of islands off the coast of Asia Minor. The Spartans were overwhelmingly defeated. They lost 70 ships, and a Spartan general, Callicratidas, was killed.

But the victory was not completely satisfying to Athens. Twenty-five Athenian ships had been lost. And hundreds of Athenian soldiers, floating in the water near their sinking ships, had been allowed to drown while the Athenian generals argued about strategy. Eight men had replaced Alcibiades; they held joint command, and by the time they had decided what to do after the battle, the seas were so rough that the survivors could not be rescued.

Athens was horrified at the bungling of the eight generals. They had beaten the Spartans, yes, but they had needlessly let Athenian citizens drown, and they had also let many Spartans escape after the battle. There was angry muttering against the eight generals. Two of them, Protomachus and Aristogenes, guessed what was about to happen, and fled into exile. The other six returned to Athens and were promptly arrested.

It was an ugly moment for Athens. The generals, after all, had won an important victory. It was too bad that men had drowned while the generals argued, but war was war; this was no way to treat victorious leaders!

None the less, they were brought to trial. The relatives of the men who had drowned appeared in public dressed in black, heads shaven in mourning. They demanded vengeance against the generals. An angry mob shouted for the death of the unhappy men. The Athenian Assembly let itself be stampeded by the fury of the mob. The Assembly voted to settle the fate of the generals, not before a regular court, but in the Assembly itself. That was illegal by Athenian laws. Furthermore, the Assembly said, all eight generals would be tried in a group. Their fates would be decided jointly, not in eight individual trials. This, too, went against Athenian law. Perhaps one or two of the generals had done all in their power to save the drowning men. Should they be condemned along with the guilty generals?

Before the Assembly could act, its steering body, the Council of Five Hundred, had to prepare a resolution. The Council, as earlier noted, was divided into ten committees, of 50 men each, which took turns throughout the year. The chairmanships of the committees changed hands every day, with a different man presiding each 24 hours.

On the day that the matter of the generals came to a vote, the chairman of the Council was Socrates.

He had never taken any part in politics. "I am too honest to be a politician," he often said. "If I took part in public affairs, I would not be allowed to live very long."

But Socrates was above all else a good citizen. He served his polis whenever his polis demanded. Time and again, he went to battle, though he could not have loved war; and when it was his turn to serve in the Council, he served his turn. Only a trick of fate found him in the chairman's seat on the day when a thoroughly unjust motion had to be voted on.

A Council member named Callixenus delivered a fiery attack on the eight generals. He demanded that all eight be brought to trial in a single group and sentenced to death. The discussion was long and heated.

"This motion is illegal," declared Socrates firmly, as chairman. "The generals must be tried separately."

The clamor of the angry mob could be heard in the streets. Callixenus repeated the accusations against the generals and asked for a vote. "Whoever opposes this motion," he cried, "is a traitor to Athens!"

Socrates continued to protest. He pretended he had not

heard the request for a vote, and tried to keep the matter from coming to a decision. But he was overwhelmed. The Council ignored its chairman and voted as Callixenus wanted. Only Socrates, of all those present, voted against the measure.

"Impeach him!" someone cried. "Arrest him! Arrest the traitor Socrates!"

No one, however, tried to arrest Socrates. He was allowed to go his way in peace. As for the generals, they were sentenced to death, and the six who had been so unwise as to return to Athens were executed immediately. One of them was Pericles, the only surviving son of the great Pericles.

The Athenian victory at Arginusae had put Athens back on top in the struggle for supremacy. Sparta once again asked for peace. The Athenians, with short memories forgetful of how close they had come to destruction in 411, rejected the bid. Puffed up with pride, Athens launched new attacks on the Spartans. Success gave way to abrupt calamity. In the summer of 405, the Spartan general Lysander trapped the Athenian fleet and all but destroyed it, at a place called Aegospotami. Only nine Athenian ships, out of 180, escaped. The Spartans captured 160 Athenian ships to add to their own navy. Lysander put 3,000 prisoners of war to death.

The Peloponnesian War was over. It had dragged on for 26 years, and it ended suddenly in a single battle. Athens had suffered such a severe defeat at Aegospotami that she could no longer resist.

Thucydides, the Athenian historian of the war, wrote, "It was at night that a ship arrived at Athens with tidings of the disaster, and a sound of wailing ran from the Piraeus through the long walls to the city, one man passing on the news to another. During that night no one slept, all mourning, not for the lost men alone, but far more for themselves, thinking that they would now suffer such treatment as they had given the Melians and many other Greek people." The next day, the Assembly met and voted to blockade the harbors and prepare Athens for a siege.

The Spartans closed in on Athens. Without food, without ships, without allies, the Athenians were helpless. They began to starve, while the Spartans waited patiently. At last, with famine clutching them, the Athenians sent an ambassador to King Agis of Sparta, who was camped near the city walls.

Athens offered to become the ally of Sparta, if only she could be allowed to keep her walls. The Spartans replied that Athens must surrender and allow her walls to be torn down. Corinth, Thebes, and other enemies of Athens felt that even that was too merciful; they asked for the total destruction of Athens. Finally, terms were decided. Athens could have peace if she surrendered all but 12 of her remaining ships, tore down her walls, allowed her pro-Spartan exiles to come home, and vowed loyalty to Sparta.

With Athenians dying from hunger every day, there was no choice but to give in. On the 16th of April, 404, Lysander entered Athens in triumph, and workmen began to rip down the walls that had guarded the proud city for so long.

Socrates was 66 years old. He had seen Athens grow great under Pericles, and he had lived to see Athens suffer this woeful defeat and humiliation. It was a sad day for Athens when Spartan soldiers paraded through her streets, but it could have come as no surprise to Socrates. He knew that, while Pericles had made Athens great, he had not been able to make her wise. Swollen with pride, hungry for power and wealth, Athens had turned away from the path of wisdom to seek an empire—and this was the price she now had to pay.

The old democratic constitution of Athens went onto the scrapheap. Lysander established a new form of government. For the time being, the Spartan general declared, Athens would be ruled by a Commission of Thirty. The Thirty would rule until they worked out a permanent system of government to replace the democracy.

And who were the Thirty? They were exiles, aristocrats who had always hated democracy in Athens, men who had fled to Sparta years ago and were returning to take charge. Each of Athens' ten tribes was supposed to pick three men to serve on the new commission. Actually, though, the Thirty were hand-picked to serve the interests of Sparta.

The leader of the Thirty was a man named Critias. Critias once had been a disciple of Socrates, and a lover of philosophy. But that had been a long time ago. Along with Alcibiades, Critias had been mixed up in the scandal of the mutilated hermae, and had been exiled from Athens. Now he was eager to grab power and ruin those who had opposed him. He acted as if he did not remember a single shred of the things Socrates had said about justice, virtue and wisdom.

Critias shared power in the defeated city with Theramenes, a man who had taken part in the battle of Arginusae in 406. Theramenes had been a junior officer then, and it was he who first raised the outcry against the eight bungling generals. Perhaps Theramenes himself had been responsible for letting the soldiers drown, and he had been protecting himself by accusing his superiors. In any event, he was the one who had led the fight against the convicted generals.

Critias, Theramenes, and the rest of the Thirty took charge of Athens late in 404. Absent from their number was Alcibiades. He had changed sides so often that nobody trusted him. Sparta had condemned him to death when the war ended, and he had fled to Persia. The Spartans persuaded the Persians to put him to death. Alcibiades was hunted down in an obscure village, and died fighting. His death came in 404, the same year that Athenian freedom perished. He was forty-six years old, and all his brilliant promise had come to nothing.

The Thirty began a reign of terror. First they slew the men responsible for exiling them. Then they began to execute political opponents who might restore the democracy. Soon the Thirty were putting Athenians to death for purely personal reasons. They might have a man executed because someone on the Thirty coveted his house, or because he had once had a private feud with one of the new rulers.

As the butchery continued, many democratic Athenians fled in horror from the city. They moved to the nearby Piraeus, which became the headquarters for enemies of the Thirty. Socrates, though, remained in Athens. No matter what changes his beloved city underwent, he would not leave it.

Surprisingly, the Thirty did not direct their bloodthirstiness against Socrates. Many Athenians who were regarded as possible troublemakers were put to death or driven into exile; but Socrates, the arch troublemaker of them all, was left in peace. Why?

Perhaps because Socrates had never been too closely associated with the overthrown Athenian democracy. He had never held public office, except for his service in the Assembly, which every citizen had to contribute. And he had often been critical of the old regime. While all men had praised the great Pericles, Socrates had pointed out that he and the other statesmen of the democracy had "filled the city full of harbors and docks and walls and revenues and all that, and left no room for justice and temperance." In fact, Socrates had gone so far as to say that when disorder came to Athens, "the people will blame the advisers of the hour, and applaud Themistocles [a leader of Athens in the war against Persia] and Cimon and Pericles, who are the real authors of their calamities."

So possibly Critias and his fellow tyrants felt that Socrates was on their side, since he had spoken out against the old government. Or maybe Critias simply did not have the heart to attack his wise old friend.

Indeed, Socrates seems to have led a charmed life during the terrifying reign of the Thirty. He was possibly the only man who openly defied the tyrants and got away with it.

This happened when the Thirty decided to put to death a certain businessman named Leon of Salamis. Apparently he went on the list of the doomed for no other reason than that the Thirty wanted to confiscate his property. The Thirty picked five Athenian citizens and ordered them to arrest Leon. And one of the five was Socrates.

The order, Socrates thought, was plainly illegal. He knew that the Thirty had chosen him for the job because they hoped in that way to involve him in their bloody crimes. So instead of going to Salamis to arrest Leon, Socrates simply ignored the order and went home. The other four citizens obediently fetched Leon, who was duly put to death.

Socrates was not punished for his disobedience. Possibly the influence of Charmides, Plato's uncle and a member of the Thirty, saved him. For Charmides, like Critias, had once been part of Socrates' little circle of disciples.

Now there was conflict among the Thirty. Theramenes, one of the original ringleaders, was appalled at the growing lawlessness of his fellow tyrants. In only a few months, 1,500 Athenians had been put to death by the Thirty, and some 5,000 had been banished. Nor had the Thirty done anything about drawing up a new constitution. They acted as though they intended to rule this way forever.

Theramenes spoke out against Critias and demanded that the rule of law be restored. Critias reacted by having Theramenes' name removed from the list of citizens. Then the Thirty condemned Theramenes to death. He was given a cup of poison to drink, and managed a grim joke as he quaffed it: "I drink to the health of the gentle Critias," he said.

Now the terror was on in earnest. Many shocked Athenians, fearing that their turn to drink Critias' health soon would come, joined the exiles in the Piraeus. A man named Thrasybulus arose as the leader of the exiled democrats. In December, 404, he set out for Athens with only 70 men, and seized a mountain fort on the borders of the city. Volunteers joined him there. The Thirty sent Spartan soldiers against Thrasybulus' growing army, but the Spartans were ambushed by night and slain.

The rebels moved closer to Athens. Critias led an army against them, but Thrasybulus and his men were firmly entrenched. As Critias and a force of 1,000 hoplites climbed the hill toward them, a shower of arrows drove them back. Critias and Charmides were killed.

The power of the Thirty was broken. The surviving tyrants fled to the city of Eleusis, and the reign of terror ended in February, 403, after eight frightening months.

Thrasybulus entered the city. But new fighting broke out, between rich and poor, and not until August was order restored.

Weary Athens, shattered by a disastrous war and by the cruelty of the Thirty, emerged now from her time of confusion. She took advantage of a disagreement among her conquerors, Sparta and Corinth and Thebes, to re-establish the democracy. All the political exiles were called home, all but the Thirty. The old laws, the laws of Solon, were revived. Once again there would be an Assembly, and a Council of Five Hundred. There would be regular courts, and justice for all. The old Athens, the wonderful lost Athens of wisdom and tolerance, was to be brought back to life.

It was a glorious moment. After all the tragedy of the war, it seemed like a miracle that Athens would rise like the phoenix from her own ashes, wiser because of her defeat. And in that moment of miracles, in that restored democracy, in that reborn polis, a strange thing happened.

Socrates was put on trial on a charge of impiety. The man who had defied the tyrants and lived was brought up to face trial and possibly a penalty of death.

12

❖ ❖ ❖

The Trial of Socrates

IT HAPPENED LATE in the year 400. The democracy had
been restored three years before, but so much confusion
had existed that it had taken all this time for the new
government to get around to dealing with Socrates.

The man who led the campaign against Socrates was a
politician named Anytus. He had been a friend of Theramenes, whom Critias had put to death. Now Anytus was
one of the most important men in the new government,
second only to Thrasybulus.

Anytus was basically an honest and thoughtful man. He
had watched the crumbling of Athens; he had seen the old
way of life disappear, and had witnessed how Athens had
become a murderous and lawless place. Anytus thought he
knew why it had happened. It was the fault of all the sophists and philosophers who had swarmed through the city,
criticizing things. The philosophers had not been content

with society as it existed. They were always hunting for flaws, poking holes. They had brought about, so Anytus thought, a general religious and moral collapse. Thanks to them, he maintained, Athens had been an easy victim to the violent, greedy, proud men who had ruled her.

And who was the greatest critic of them all? Who was the one who went around the city raising all manner of worrisome questions? Who, more than anyone else, had left Athenians disturbed and uncertain about things?

Why, Socrates, of course!

Socrates was dangerous. He had great influence among young men, and he was forever stirring them up, filling their heads with strange thoughts. Just look at who Socrates' pupils had been! Alcibiades, for one—that drunken rowdy who had entangled Athens in the crazy expedition to Sicily. If any man had brought Athens to ruin, it was Alcibiades, the close friend of Socrates. Then there were Critias and Charmides, two more members of Socrates' little circle of friends. They had been members of the Thirty, hadn't they? They had been bloody-handed tyrants. That was the sort of man Socrates gave the city. If he went on, talking in his strange way to the young people, who knew but that he might not bring forth some new Alcibiades, some new Critias?

Anytus sincerely felt that it was necessary for the good of Athens that Socrates go. He did not particularly want the old man put to death. He merely believed that Socrates must go into exile—the farther from Athens, the better.

But Anytus could not bring charges against Socrates on the grounds that his friends had been members of the Thirty. The political amnesty of 403 had insured that; nobody could be prosecuted merely for associating with the Thirty. So Anytus found a subtler way of attacking Socrates.

He persuaded a young religious fanatic named Meletus to bring charges of impiety against Socrates. The same thing had been done long before, to get rid of the philosopher Anaxagoras. Since the political charges against Anaxagoras—that he was in conspiracy with Persia—could not be proved, he was tried for impiety and offenses against the gods, and forced into exile.

The indictment drawn up by Meletus was this: "Socrates is guilty of not worshiping the gods whom the city worships, and of bringing in strange gods. He is also guilty of corrupting the young men of the city."

At long last, Socrates was in deep trouble with the government. All his life he had gone his own way, unafraid of making himself unpopular. He had pursued truth without regard for the dangers. Men had mocked him, as Aristophanes had done long ago in *The Clouds,* but men had never before tried to take legal action against him.

Even in the dangerous times of the rule of the Thirty, Socrates had gone right on asking his questions and challenging the established way of things. He alone in all of Athens seemed to have no fear of the 30 tyrants. When one of them, Charicles, warned Socrates to stop asking questions of young men, Socrates had replied blithely, "Suppose I want to buy something, am I not even allowed to ask the price if the seller is under thirty?"

"You can ask that kind of question, yes," said Charicles. "But you are in the habit of asking questions to which you know the answer, so that is what you are not to do."

Socrates had shrugged the warning off and continued to ask. Perhaps the Thirty would have had to do away with the annoying old man eventually. But they had fallen from power before they could harm him. Now it was the democracy itself that sought to seal Socrates' lips.

The charge of Meletus first went to the nine archons of Athens. One in particular, known as the King Archon, heard preliminary testimony from the accuser and the accused. It was while going to the hall of the King Archon that Socrates had his meeting with Euthyphro, in which they discussed the nature of piety. Even now, with his life at stake, Socrates could not resist asking questions.

The trial itself began in February, 399. Under Athenian law, there was no presiding judge; 501 Athenian citizens, chosen by lot, would decide the guilt or innocence of Socrates, and they would determine his fate if convicted. There was no fixed penalty for impiety; the jury could select any punishment it wanted.

The accusers spoke first. They presented the case against Socrates: he worshiped strange gods, he did not believe in the gods of Athens, and he taught young men to think dangerous thoughts.

The charge of not believing in the gods of Athens was a very serious one. To an Athenian, religion was more than a matter of prayer and ritual. It was part of the fabric of the polis. Religious feeling and patriotism were intertwined. A man who did not worship Athena or Apollo was failing to express his loyalty to the entire polis. It was not necessary to believe all the old stories about the doings of Zeus and Hermes and Apollo and the rest. But it *was* necessary to attend the festivals of the gods, to take part in the religious ceremonies, and to visit the temples. In that way, a man showed that he was a true member of the polis.

When the prosecution had finished, Socrates rose to speak in his own defense. "They have said I am a clever speaker," he told the jurors. "They have warned you not to let me deceive you. But you will see that I am not a clever speaker at all, unless by a clever speaker they mean a man who speaks the truth. My accusers have said little or nothing that is true, but from me you shall hear the whole truth."

He apologized for his lack of skill with legal phrases. "I am more than seventy years old," he said, "and this is the first time that I have ever come before a law court. So your manner of speech here is quite strange to me. But never mind the manner of my speech, give your whole attention to the question, Is what I say just, or is it not?"

He began by declaring that he had two sets of accusations to face: the current charges, and also older charges that went as far back as *The Clouds* of Aristophanes. Socrates chose to deal with the older charges first. They were more serious, he said, because they had been circulating since some of the jurors were children, and so the jurors were likely to believe they were true.

"My old accusers have persuaded you that there is a certain Socrates, a wise man, who speculates about the heavens, and who investigates things that are beneath the earth, and who can make the worse argument appear the stronger. They say that persons who study such things never believe in the gods. I cannot tell you who these accusers are, except one who happens to be a comic poet. In the comedy of Aristophanes you yourselves saw a man called Socrates swinging around in a basket and saying that he walked the air, and sputtering a great deal of nonsense about matters of which I understand nothing. The truth is, Athenians, I have nothing to do with these matters."

Looking about the courtroom, he asked if anyone had ever heard him discussing such things. The charge, he said, was false. So, too, was another popular claim, that Socrates took money to educate men. "I think it would be a fine thing to be able to educate men," he said. "But I do not have that skill, and so I have never made money by teaching."

But if he did not teach for money, and he did not study the heavens and the earth, what *did* he do? To answer that, Socrates reviewed the whole course of his life. He told of Chaerephon's visit to the Oracle, and how he himself had gone about the city afterward, looking for a wise man. He explained his mission—to show others that their wisdom was hollow. "People suppose I am wise myself in those things in which I convict another of ignorance. They are mistaken. The god alone is wise, and his Oracle declares that human wisdom is worth little or nothing. That man is wisest who like Socrates knows that he is worthless so far as wisdom is concerned. The disgraceful ignorance is to think you know what you do not know."

And, he added, "I am so busy in this pursuit that I have never had leisure to take any part worth mentioning in public matters or to look after my private affairs. I am in great poverty as the result of my service to the gods."

Next Socrates turned to the present charges: first, the charge of corrupting the youth of Athens.

"Come here, Meletus," Socrates said.

Socrates' accuser made a serious mistake: he stepped forward and allowed Socrates to question him. The simple-minded fanatic was no equal to Socrates at this game.

"Come, tell us, my good man, who is it who improves the young people?"

"The laws."

"That, my friend, is not the question. What *person* improves the young of Athens?"

"The judges here, Socrates."

"All of them? Or only some of them?"

"All of them."

"By Hera, that is good news! Such a large supply of benefactors! And do the listeners here improve them, or not?"

"They do."

"And do the members of the Council?"

"Yes."

"And do the members of the Assembly corrupt the young, or do they again all improve them?"

"They, too, improve them," said Meletus.

"Then all the Athenians, apparently, make the young into good men except me, and I alone corrupt them. Is that your meaning?"

"Most certainly that is my meaning."

"Now tell me," said Socrates. "Do you think that the same holds good in the case of horses? Does one man do them harm and everyone else improve them? On the contrary, only a very few, those who are skilled with horses, can improve them, while the majority of men harm them if they use them. How lucky the young people are, then, if only one man corrupted them, and everyone else did them good!"

Meletus sputtered in bewilderment. Some of the jurors no doubt chuckled as Socrates spun his web.

Socrates asked, "Are you prosecuting me for corrupting the young and making them worse voluntarily, or involuntarily?"

"For doing it voluntarily," answered Meletus.

"What, Meletus? Do you mean to say that you, who are so much younger than I, are so much wiser than I? Do you think I don't know that if I went about the city doing evil voluntarily, someone would certainly injure me? Either I do not corrupt the young at all or I do so involuntarily. You are lying in either case, then. And if I corrupt them involuntarily, you should not prosecute me for my error, but take me aside privately and reprove and educate me. For, of course, I shall cease to do wrong involuntarily, as soon as I know that I have been doing wrong."

While Meletus puzzled over that, Socrates went on to discuss the charge that he was corrupting the young by teaching the worship of new gods to replace the familiar gods of Athens.

"Explain yourself more clearly," Socrates said. "Do you mean that I teach the young to believe in strange gods, or that I am a complete atheist, and teach other people not to believe in any gods at all?"

The second idea sounded much more wicked to Meletus, so he seized it. "I mean that you do not believe in the gods in any way whatever," he blurted.

"You amaze me, Meletus! Why do you say that? Do you mean that I believe neither the sun nor the moon to be gods, as other men believe?"

"I swear he does not, judges. He says that the sun is a stone, and the moon is dirt!"

"My dear Meletus," said Socrates, smiling, "do you think you are prosecuting Anaxagoras?"

"You are a complete atheist," the confused Meletus shouted.

Socrates pounced eagerly. "In your original charge, you swore that I believe in divine beings, whether old gods or new. Now you say that I believe in no gods at all. You contradict yourself. It seems to me, Athenians, that Meletus is a very insolent and wanton man, and that he is prosecuting me simply in the insolence and wantonness of youth. You must have indicted me in this manner, Meletus, either to test my skill, or because you could not find any crime that you could accuse me of with truth."

He let the unhappy Meletus sit down. The charge of atheism, Socrates said, was so feeble it was not even worth discussing. Everyone knew he was a pious man who believed in the gods of the polis. Only in that mocking play of Aristophanes had he seemed to be denying the divinity of Zeus. The real Socrates had never said any such thing.

Socrates explained that he had always acted in the way he thought was right. The fear of death had never troubled him. That was why, instead of taking the easy way out and going into voluntary exile, he had chosen to stand trial. "When the generals whom you chose to command me, Athenians, assigned me my station at Potidaea and at Amphipolis and at Delium, I remained where they stationed me and ran the risk of death, like other men. It would be very strange conduct on my part if I were to desert my post now from fear of death or any other thing, when God has commanded me—as I am persuaded that he has done—to spend my life in searching for wisdom, and in examining myself and others."

So he openly defied the jury. Do not think, he told them, that he would change his ways if acquitted! He would make no deals to gain his freedom. "As long as I have breath and strength," he said, "I will not give up philosophy and exhorting you and declaring the truth to every one of you whom I meet." For so the gods had ordered him to do.

He warned the jury not to act foolishly. Athens, he said, needed him. He had been sent by the gods to play a vital role in the life of the city.

"For if you kill me," he said, "you will not easily find a successor to me. I am a sort of gadfly, given to the state by

God; and the state is a great and noble steed who is slow in his motions because of his very size, and needs to be stirred into life. I am that gadfly which God has attached to the state, and all day long I am constantly alighting upon you, arousing and persuading and reproaching you. You will not easily find another like me, and therefore I would advise you to spare my life."

Socrates observed that his service to Athens had won him no personal advantage, for he was a poor man. His poverty was the best witness to his honesty. He had served Athens in his own way, heedless of personal danger. He reminded the jury how he had defied the mob that had screamed for the lives of the generals of Arginusae. He spoke of his refusal to arrest Leon of Salamis.

"I do not care a straw for death," he said, "but I do care very much indeed about not doing anything unjust and impious."

What about the charge that Alcibiades and Critias had been his pupils? False, Socrates said. "I was never anyone's teacher, so no one was my pupil. I am ready to ask questions of rich and poor alike, and if any man wishes to answer me, and then listen to what I have to say, he may. But I cannot be blamed if those men turn out bad, nor praised if they turn out good, for I never taught or claimed to teach any of them any knowledge whatever."

He had said nearly all he wanted to say in his own defense. He remarked now that some men, when on trial, brought their weeping wives and children to court to make the jurors feel pity. "I shall do none of these things," he said. "I have three sons, one of them a lad, and the other two still children. Yet I will not bring any of them forward before you and beg you to acquit me." A judge, he observed, does not **give away** justice as a favor. Socrates wanted to be judged according to the law, and no other way.

"For I do believe that there are gods," he said in conclusion. "I believe in the gods as no one of my accusers believes in them. And to you and to God I commit my cause, to be decided as is best for you and for me."

Socrates took his seat. The judges prepared to vote. It was a secret ballot, and it took a while for all the votes to be counted. The 501 jurors, many of whom had known Socrates for years, had heard the prosecution, and had listened to Socrates' speech of defense, and now they had to decide a verdict: had he taught false gods? Had he corrupted the young men? Was he dangerous to Athens?

The votes were tallied. Socrates was found guilty, by a vote of 281 to 220.

Athens, grown fearful and intolerant, had pronounced its verdict on Socrates. He was a dangerous man, a subversive, a troublemaker. Now the punishment had to be determined.

Where the laws of Athens prescribed no fixed penalty for a crime, the punishment was determined in a sort of bargaining process. The prosecutor suggested one penalty and the convicted man suggested another one, naturally a milder one. The jury then chose one or the other.

Meletus asked for the death penalty. Quite probably neither he nor his backer, Anytus, expected to get it. Almost certainly they thought that Socrates would propose exile as the alternative, and that the jury would vote for that choice.

But Socrates, as usual, did the unexpected. He rose to speak, and there was a hush in the great hall. It was a sad moment for Socrates, but not really a surprising one. He had known all along that he had many enemies in Athens. At last, his enemies had turned on him and defeated him.

"I am not indignant at your verdict, Athenians," he said. "I expected you would find me guilty, and the only thing that surprises me is the numbers of the votes. I certainly never thought that the majority against me would have been so narrow. But now it seems that if only some thirty votes had changed sides, I should have escaped."

He turned to the matter of the penalty. Meletus wanted him to die. Socrates was well aware that if he asked for banishment, that would be his sentence. But it went against his principles to do that. It would be an admission of guilt, and he felt guilty of nothing. He refused to bargain with the jury. If they would not free him outright, let them put him to death.

He spoke with heavy irony. "So Meletus proposes death as the penalty, Athenians. Be it so. And what alternative penalty shall I propose to you? What I deserve, of course, must I not? What then do I deserve to pay or to suffer, for having determined not to spend my life in ease? I neglected the things which most men value, such as wealth, and family interests, and military commands, and all the political appointments, and clubs. I did not go where I should have done no good to you or to myself. Instead, I went where I could do the greatest good privately to every one of you, and sought to persuade every man among you that he must look to himself, and seek virtue and wisdom before he looks to his private interests."

What does such a man deserve for living and acting that way, Socrates asked? "Something good, Athenians. A suitable reward to be given to a poor man who is your benefactor, and who desires leisure that he may instruct you."

Socrates suggested that he be given free meals for the

rest of his life at the expense of the polis. That was a reward given to famous generals, victors at the Olympic games, and other celebrities.

He was openly mocking the court. He had been asked to name a punishment for his deeds, and instead he had named a reward. An angry stir ran through the rows of jurors. Had the man no sense? Why was he jeering at them at a time like this, the jurors asked? Why not simply ask for exile, instead of angering them with this sarcasm?

It was nothing but contempt of court. Socrates knew that. He had only wanted to make the point one last time that he was innocent, and deserved well of Athens, not harm. "I am convinced I never wronged any man voluntarily, though I cannot persuade you of that for we have discussed together for only a short time. I shall certainly not admit that I deserve to suffer any evil, or propose any evil as a penalty for myself. Why should I? Shall I propose imprisonment, and spend the rest of my days in jail? Or shall I propose a fine? I have no money to pay a fine with. Shall I propose exile? No, indeed. A fine life I should lead for an old man if I were to withdraw from Athens and pass the rest of my days in wandering from city to city, and always being expelled. For if my fellow citizens cast me out, would strangers not do the same to me?"

He asked himself, "Why can't you withdraw from Athens and hold your peace, Socrates?" And he answered: "That would be to disobey the gods. I tell you that no greater good can happen to a man than to discuss virtue every day, and the other matters about which you have heard me arguing. An unexamined life is not worth living."

While Socrates was delivering these words, his friends were holding a hurried conference. They saw that if he kept talking in this vein, he was certain to be given a death sentence. So four wealthy disciples of Socrates—Crito, Critobulus, Apollodorus, and Plato—agreed to put up 30 minae of silver as a fine for Socrates.

That was a large amount of money. It took an ordinary workingman about six months to earn a single mina. But a fine, no matter how big, would not silence Socrates. He would still be there in Athens, still asking his questions, still corrupting young minds. So the choice he had given the jury was no choice at all. Death or a fine—and the jury had to pick the penalty that would rid Athens of the old man. The jurors voted to put Socrates to death. The vote against him this time was even larger: 360 to 141. The mocking tone of Socrates' words had angered some of those who had voted to acquit him before.

The condemned man rose to offer a few more words to the jury:

"You have not gained very much time, Athenians, and, as the price of it, you will have an evil name forever. For the enemies of Athens will say that you put Socrates, a wise man, to death. And they will certainly call me wise, whether I am wise or not, when they want to reproach you."

Mildly he suggested that they could have waited a few years, and let the course of nature remove him instead; for he was an old man, and would not in any case have remained to trouble Athens much longer.

Once again, he repeated his belief in his own innocence. He had been condemned, he said, because he had refused to weep and wail before the jury, and because he had declined to go back on his own beliefs to save his life. "I think it is a much harder thing to escape from wickedness than from death, for wickedness is swifter than death. And now I, who am old and slow, have been overtaken by the slower pursuer; and my accusers, who are clever and swift, have been overtaken by the swifter pursuer—wickedness."

He said that he would abide the verdict without bitterness for "perhaps it was right for these things to have happened." He warned, though, that future generations would call Athens to account for what they had done. They were not silencing Socrates by killing him; they were only insuring that he would be immortal in the minds of men.

Nor was he frightened of death. He did not think death was evil. His divine sign had always warned him against evil, yet the sign had not stopped him when he left his house that morning to come to court, nor had the sign interfered with him while he addressed the jury. "My sign would certainly have opposed me," said Socrates, "if I had not been going to meet with something good."

No, he said, death was not evil. Either it was simply an eternal sleep, a peaceful rest, which an old man would appreciate, or else it was a journey to another place where souls were judged. If death were a journey, said Socrates, it meant that he would be going to another world where all the great men of Greece had gone. He would be able to spend his time in conversation with Homer and Aeschylus, with Pericles and Agamemnon, with Odysseus and Achilles. "That I think would be no small pleasure," said Socrates.

He turned to his friends in the courtroom and made one last request: that they look after his sons, and see that the lads grew up as their father would have had them grow up. "Punish them, my friends, if they seem to you to care for riches or for any other thing more than virtue. And if they think that they are something when they are really nothing, reproach them, as I have reproached you."

The trial was at its end. There was no more that the old man could say.

"The hour of departure has arrived," Socrates declared. "We go our separate ways—I to die, and you to live. Which is better is known to God alone."

13

❖ ❖ ❖

Exit Socrates—Still Talking

JUSTICE was usually swift in Athens. A condemned man was normally handed over to the executioner within 24 hours after the trial. Socrates, though, was granted a delay by luck. Each year, Athens sent a sacred ship to the shrine of Apollo, at Delos. The law of the city held that from the time the ship departed to the time of its return, no executions could be carried out in Athens.

The sacred ship had left the day before the trial of Socrates began. Weeks would pass before it returned. Socrates was put in the public prison and forced to wear chains. His jailer was a kind-hearted man who treated Socrates as well as the law allowed, permitting his friends to visit him every day.

Socrates amused himself in many ways. When his friends were with him, he discussed philosophical matters as he always had. In the lonelier hours of the night, he turned his hand to poetry for the first time. A voice in a dream had told him, "Cultivate and make music." He obeyed the dream by writing a hymn to the god Apollo, and by turning some fables of Aesop into verse.

Then, too, he could look back on his long life, reviewing for the last time the things he believed. He had never put together any system of philosophy, such as other Greek thinkers had assembled. He had only been interested in matters of good and evil, of knowledge and ignorance.

Again and again, in his many conversations, he had tried to show that virtue was knowledge, that a man must strive for understanding and wisdom if he hopes to be good. This knowledge, Socrates had said many times, could not be taught in classroom lectures. A man could not know that what others call right and good is really so, unless he saw it for himself. And he could only see it by examining himself, by questioning every belief, by striving to see through the mists of prejudice and confusion. "An unexamined life," Socrates had said at his trial, "is not worth living."

But what if a man attained this knowledge, and refused to live by it? Impossible, Socrates said. No one knowingly does wrong. The man of true wisdom will always act virtuously. A man who does evil is merely misled and mistaken. So Socrates did not feel that his jurors had condemned him for evil reasons. They were simply confused men, he said, who did not really know right from wrong.

Finally, Socrates had insisted, happiness is the result of goodness. The wicked man is never truly happy, even when stuffing himself with food, even when enjoying his riches to the utmost. Had Alcibiades been happy—that lonely, exiled man? Had the tyrants of the Thirty been happy? No, because their lives had been choked with fear. One who lives by oppressing others can never feel the true happiness of a virtuous man. One who lives righteously is happy, though he undergoes poverty, suffering and death.

And so Socrates, the condemned man, chained in his cell and waiting to die, was a happy man, perhaps the happiest in Athens, because he had lived a virtuous life and had no apologies to make to anyone.

The days passed. Crito, the wealthiest of Socrates' friends, tried to get the old man released on bail until the sacred ship returned, but the offer was refused by the court. The despairing disciples met with one another endlessly, trying to work out some way of saving Socrates, who was indifferent to their efforts. Such men as Plato and Crito, and young Phaedo of Elis, and two Theban disciples, Simmias and Cebes, visited the old man often, but he was always in better spirits than they.

Toward the end of the month, Socrates had a visitor at daybreak. Socrates woke to find Crito standing by his cot.

"How is it the jailer let you in?" Socrates asked.

"He knows me, Socrates. I come here so often. Besides, he owed me a favor." Crito did not want to say that he had bribed the jailer.

"Have you been here long?"

"Yes. Some time."

"Why didn't you wake me?"

"You were sleeping so sweetly, Socrates. How easily and calmly you bear the calamity that has come to you!"

"Nay, Crito, it would be absurd if at my age I were disturbed at having to die."

"Other men just as old are overtaken by similar calamities, Socrates. But their age does not save them from being disturbed with their fate."

"That is so," agreed Socrates. "But tell me, why are you here so early?"

Crito replied that he was the bearer of bitter news: the sacred ship was due to return from Delos in another day or two, and Socrates would have to die the day after its arrival. All month, Crito had been begging Socrates to escape from prison; now there was no more time to waste.

"For no very large sum we could buy your safety," said Crito. "My fortune is at your service. And if you have any feeling about making use of my money, there are strangers in Athens whom you know, ready to use theirs." Simmias and Cebes, the two Thebans, were prepared to make the necessary bribes. Since they were not Athenians, they would run no risks by obtaining his release, while a fellow-citizen like Crito could be tried for interfering with the laws of the polis.

"There are many places for you to go to, Socrates, where you will be welcomed," Crito said. "If you choose to go to Thessaly, I have friends there who will make much of you, and shelter you. And besides, Socrates, I think that you will be doing what is wrong if you abandon your life when you might preserve it. You are simply playing the game of your enemies; it is exactly the game of those who wanted to destroy you." Crito reminded Socrates of his small children; was it right to depart from the world without taking the trouble of bringing them up and educating them? "It seems to me that you are choosing the easy way, and not the way of a good and brave man, as you ought, when you have been talking all your life long of the value that you set upon virtue."

Crito declared that the time for discussion was past. "Everything must be done tonight. If we delay any longer, we are lost."

Socrates had listened to all this without a word. Now he replied, thanking Crito for his anxiety to save him. But, said Socrates, we must consider—is it right to do as Crito wished, or is it wrong?

Socrates began to question his friend. "Do we still hold to the belief that we should set the highest value, not on living, but on living well?"

"Yes, we do."

"And living well and honorably and justly mean the same thing. Do we hold to that or not?"

"We do."

"Then we have to consider," said Socrates, "whether it is just or not for me to try to escape from prison without the consent of the Athenians. If we find that it is just, we will try; if not, we will abstain. I'm afraid that considerations of expense, and of reputation, and of bringing up my children, are beside the point."

Crito agreed that Socrates would not be honorable to act unjustly. And, he admitted, it was unjust to repay evil with evil, injustice with injustice.

Socrates posed an imaginary question. Suppose the laws and the polis were to come to him, he said, and ask, "Tell us, Socrates, what have you in your mind to do? What do you mean by trying to escape? Are you trying to destroy the laws and the polis? Do you think a state can exist if private individuals disregard its laws?"

Would it be right, he wondered, to answer, "But the state has injured me, it has decided my case unjustly."

No, he said. For the laws could reply, "Was that our agreement? Or was it that you would submit to whatever judgment the state should pronounce?"

By living all his life in Athens, Socrates told Crito, he had voluntarily made himself subject to the laws of Athens. If he had been dissatisfied with those laws, he could have gone to some other city long ago. Furthermore, he could have fled into exile when charges first were brought against him, but he had chosen to stay and stand trial. That implied an agreement to abide by the decision of the court.

He could not break that agreement now, and run away "like a miserable slave." If he escaped now, he would be flouting the laws of Athens, doing the very thing his accusers had condemned him for doing. A man who defies the law also might well be a corrupter of the young, an enemy of the gods. How could he go on talking about virtue and justice, having done such a thing?

"Can I go off to your friends in Thessaly?" he asked. "Can I let people say that an old man, with only a few more years to live, clung so greedily to life that he dared to transgress the highest laws? I will hear much that will make me blush, if I do that."

Socrates looked steadily at his friend. "This is how I feel," he said. "I am sure that if you try to change my mind you will speak in vain. But if you think you will succeed, speak on."

"I can say no more, Socrates," Crito replied.

"Then let it be, Crito, and let us do as I say, seeing that God so directs."

In another few days, the sacred ship returned, and the time came for Socrates' sentence to be carried out. On the last morning of the philosopher's life, his friends and family began to assemble in the prison cell. Crito was there, and his son Critobulus; the Thebans—Simmias and Cebes —were present; so were Phaedo of Elis, and Echecrates of Phlios, and Ctesippus, the Athenian, and half a dozen more. Of all of Socrates' surviving disciples, only young Plato, who was more deeply devoted to Socrates than anyone, was unable to be there. Plato was ill that morning.

The jailer had taken off Socrates' chains. When the friends entered, they found Xanthippe, the wife of Socrates, sitting beside him, holding their youngest child in her arms. As she saw them, she cried, "Oh, Socrates, this is the last time that you will be able to converse with your friends!" And she began to weep and beat herself in grief.

Socrates turned calmly to Crito. "Crito, let someone take her home," he said, and Crito gestured to a servant to lead Xanthippe away.

Sitting up on his couch, Socrates rubbed his leg, for the chains had given him a cramp. He began to speak of his project of turning Aesop's fables into verse, and Cebes the Theban remarked that only the other day the poet Evenus had remarked with interest that Socrates, who had never before written a line of poetry, should now amuse himself with verse.

Socrates explained how the idea had come to him in a dream. "Tell this to Evenus," he said, "and bid him be of good cheer. Say that I would have him come after me if he be a wise man, and not tarry."

"What?" Simmias said. "Should we tell him that you invite him to join you in death?"

"Why," said Socrates, "Evenus is a philosopher, is he not? Then he, or any man who has the spirit of philosophy, will be willing to die. But he will not take his own life for that is held to be unlawful."

"Why do you say that a man ought not to take his own life, but that the philosopher will be ready to follow the dying?" asked Cebes.

Socrates replied that men are only possessions of the gods, and do not have the right to destroy themselves, any more than one of a man's own possessions, an ox or a horse, could be allowed to take its own life. "A man should wait," said Socrates, "until God summons him, as he is now summoning me."

Cebes and Simmias could not understand how Socrates was able to face death so calmly. They themselves were grieving for him; why did he seem so relaxed?

Because, Socrates said, he had every hope of going on to a better world, where wisdom was more common among men. He had nothing to fear; he was looking forward to the voyage.

At this point Crito broke in. "I have a message from the man who is to give you the poison, Socrates. He says you are not to do much talking. Talking makes the body warm, and interferes with the action of the poison. Persons who excite themselves sometimes have to take a second or even a third dose."

Socrates shrugged. "Let him mind his business and be prepared to give the poison twice or even thrice if necessary," he said. "That is all."

And he resumed the discussion. He wanted to prove to Simmias and Cebes that there was life after death, that the soul was immortal. In his old familiar manner, Socrates began to question them. What is death, he asked? Is it not the separation of body and soul? And what was the body? Only a source of endless trouble, always needing food, always plagued by diseases and aches and pains. It was better to shed one's body, since it hinders one in the search after truth.

"Yes," said Cebes, "but suppose that when the body perishes, the soul also ceases to exist? What if it vanishes like a puff of smoke in the air?"

"Perhaps," said Socrates, "it does. Shall we talk a little about whether such a thing is likely to happen?"

"I'd greatly like to know your opinion," said Cebes.

Socrates laughed. "I think that no one who heard me now could accuse me of idle talking about matters in which I have no concern. Not even my old enemies, the comic poets, could say that!"

Using all the skill at his command, Socrates set out to prove that the soul was immortal. Questioning Simmias and Cebes, he built up one of his wonderful webs of argument, trying to show why he was certain of an afterlife. He spoke beautifully and persuasively.

But it is impossible really to prove anything about life after death, and Socrates knew that as well as anyone in the room. All one could do was make guesses; no certain knowledge was possible. So eventually Socrates came to the end of his argument, and there was silence in the room. Everyone there knew that nothing had actually been settled.

"Well?" said Socrates. "What do you think of the argument? Have we left anything out? I'm sure there are still many points open to suspicion and attack."

Simmias shifted uneasily. "Yes, Socrates, there are many doubts in our minds. But we hesitate to raise questions at a time like this."

Smiling, Socrates said, "Can't you see? I don't regard my present situation as a misfortune! Can I not persuade you that I am no worse off now than at any other time in my life?"

The friends of Socrates nodded in agreement. Encouraged by Socrates, they began to raise objections to the ideas Socrates had expressed about the afterlife. And he answered them, defending his belief, correcting their errors of reasoning.

After a long discussion, Socrates began to tell them about a vision he had had, a vision of the upper earth. It was his old vision, the one he had spoken of that night at the home of Cephalus, when he told the story of the shadows on the cave wall.

"There is a world beyond our world," said Socrates. "And, if men could see it, they would know that this other world is the place of the true heaven and the true light and the true earth. Compared to it, our earth, and the stones, and our whole world, are spoiled and rusted, as in the sea where all things are rusted by the brine. Nor is there anything noble or perfect in our world, but only caverns, and sand, and mud."

In the upper world, said Socrates, "everything that grows—trees and flowers and fruits—are fairer than anything here. There are hills whose stones are smoother and lovelier than our highly valued emeralds and jaspers and sardonyxes. And the men of that other world have no disease, and live much longer than we do, and all their senses are far more perfect than ours. And they have temples in which to converse with the gods, and hear their voices and receive their answers."

When the dead from our world come to the place of judgment, they are weighed on the scale of goodness, Socrates told his listeners. Some, who have lived neither well nor ill, are sent to a great lake where they are purified of their evil deeds and given a reward for such good as they may have done. Those who have committed crimes, the murderers and the enemies of the gods, are hurled into a bottomless pit. But those who have lived virtuously all their lives are allowed to go on to the upper world, where they live forever in happiness. And there, Socrates said, he hoped to go.

"Of course," he added, "I cannot be sure it really will happen this way. But I know that the soul is immortal, and that something such as I have imagined is close to the truth. So I am of good cheer about my soul, and I am ready to go on my journey to the next world, when my hour comes."

And that hour, he saw, was at hand. He excused himself from his friends, and went to bathe, so he could meet death with a clean body. Crito went with him. The rest of the friends remained behind in the cell. They could not share the calmness of Socrates. Despite all he had said, they felt only sorrow—not so much for Socrates, but for themselves, for they were about to lose their wise and good friend.

After Socrates had bathed, he came back to the cell. His wife returned, and his three sons, and some of his relatives. He spoke with them a while, giving them some instructions about what they were to do after he was gone. Then he sent them away.

Now the hour of sunset was near. Socrates and his friends fell silent. Soon the jailer entered, looking pale and unhappy. He went up to Socrates and said, "You are the noblest and best of all who ever came to this place. I must give you the poison now, but I beg you not to be angry with me. Others are to blame for this, not I." And the man burst into tears, and went out of the cell.

Socrates said to his friends, "That man has been good to me. Since I have been in prison he has always been coming to me, and at times he would talk to me—and now see how generously he sorrows on my account. We must do as he says, Crito. And therefore let the cup be brought, if the poison is ready."

"Don't hurry, Socrates," Crito said unhappily. "There's time enough. The sun is still upon the hilltops. Many a man has taken the cup late, after eating and enjoying the company of his friends."

Socrates smiled faintly. "Yes, for they think they have something to gain by delaying. But what does it matter to me, to have a few more hours of life? My life is forfeit. Do as I say, and don't refuse me."

Crito made a sign to the servant, who went out and returned after a while with the jailer. The cup of poison was ready. Athens had decreed a merciful death for Socrates. He was to drink a poison made from the dried fruit of the hemlock plant. (This hemlock is a member of the parsley family, and not related to the evergreen hemlock tree. Hemlock is a nerve poison that acts quickly and painlessly; it paralyzes the nerves that control breathing, and life stops.)

Socrates turned to the jailer. "You, my good friend, are experienced in these matters. Tell me how I am to proceed."

The man answered, "You drink, and then you walk about until your legs are heavy, and then you lie down, and the poison will act."

Without any fear in his expression, without turning pale or looking troubled, Socrates reached for the deadly cup. His time had come. He had lived more than seventy years; he had lived a virtuous life; he had never ceased to seek truth through self-examination. And Athens had repaid his devotion with a sentence of death.

As he lifted the cup, he said to the jailer, "What do you say, may I make a libation out of this cup to the gods?" For it was customary, when a man drank, to sprinkle a few drops from the cup in honor of the gods.

The jailer answered, "We only prepare, Socrates, just so much as we deem enough."

"I understand," said Socrates. "But at least I must ask the gods to prosper my journey from this to the other world. And so be it, I pray."

He put the cup to his lips, and drank the poison readily and cheerfully. His friends, who had tried hard to keep their emotions under control all this while, were no longer able to hold back their tears. Phaedo covered his face and wept; Crito had tears streaming down his face; Apollodorus broke out in loud cries of grief.

Socrates alone remained calm. "What is this strange outcry?" he asked. "I sent away the women so that they would not misbehave in this way for I have been told that a man should die in peace. Be quiet, then, and have patience."

The friends of Socrates were ashamed when they heard his words. They wiped the tears from their eyes and struggled to remain calm. Socrates walked about the cell until he felt his legs growing stiff and heavy. He lay down on his cot. The jailer approached, looked at Socrates' feet and legs, and pressed hard on one of Socrates' feet.

"Can you feel that?" the jailer asked.

"No," said Socrates.

The chill rose, from the foot of Socrates to his calf, and then to his thigh. "I am growing cold," Socrates said calmly. "When the poison reaches the heart, that will be the end."

There was silence in the cell. Socrates seemed peaceful and serene. After a while, he remembered a debt he had left unpaid. He had vowed to sacrifice a rooster to Asclepius, the god of medicine, and he had not done it.

He said, "Crito, I owe a cock to Asclepius. Will you remember to pay the debt?"

"The debt shall be paid," said Crito. "Is there anything else?"

Socrates did not answer. He had covered his face with his blanket. A moment later, there was a movement under the blanket, and then the jailer uncovered him. The eyes of Socrates were fixed and sightless. Tenderly, Crito closed them for the last time. The long journey had begun for Socrates.

"Such was the end of our friend," wrote Plato soon afterwards, "a man, I think, who was, of all the men of his time, the wisest and best and most just."

Bibliography

I HAVE NOT PRESUMED to invent any words to be spoken by Socrates and his friends in this book. Though Athens put Socrates to death, he received immortality of the highest kind, for his friend and disciple Plato set down the great philosopher's words in a series of literary masterpieces that will endure as long as men can read. I have used the writings of Plato as my chief source for what Socrates said. Sometimes I have simplified or condensed, but I have not put my own words in the mouths of Socrates and his companions.

All the dialogues of Plato are available in two thick volumes published by Random House, *The Dialogues of Plato*. The translations, by Benjamin Jowett, were done about a hundred years ago, but they are still readable and interesting. There have also been many modern translations of the various dialogues, and a number of these are available in inexpensive paperback editions.

The dialogues of Plato that are most useful for an understanding of Socrates are these:

The Apology, Crito, and *Phaedo* tell the story of the trial and death of Socrates.

The Republic states Socrates' Theory of Forms, and the parable of the shadows in the cave. But this very long dialogue also includes much political philosophy that is entirely the work of Plato.

The Symposium is Plato's account of the banquet at Agathon's where the nature of love was discussed. Of all Plato's work, this is the most entertaining.

I have also used these additional dialogues as sources for chapters in this book: *Charmides, Laches, Protagoras, Phaedrus, Euthyphro, Gorgias,* and *Theaetetus.*

There are very few books about Socrates himself, though there are many about Plato. A slim but useful book, which is not so much a biography of Socrates as an essay on his thinking, is *Socrates: the Man and His Thought,* by A. E. Taylor (Beacon Press, Boston, 1952; Anchor Books, New York, 1953).

Aristophanes' play, *The Clouds,* can be found in *The Complete Greek Drama,* Volume Two, edited by Whitney J. Oates and Eugene O'Neill, Jr. (Random House, New York, 1938).

For the historical background of Socrates' times, there are two good one-volume books, one big, one small. The big one is *The Will of Zeus,* by Stringfellow Barr (Lippincott, Philadelphia, 1961), which is a superb history of Greece and her culture from earliest times down to the death of Alexander the Great. The other book is *The Greeks,* by H. D. F. Kitto, a lively and scholarly paperback volume (Pelican Books, Harmondsworth, England, 1951).

The classic account of the war between Athens and Sparta is *The Peloponnesian War,* by Thucydides. There are many modern editions of this great book in English translation.

My own *Fifteen Battles That Changed the World* (Putnam, 1963) includes a chapter on the struggle between Greece and Persia.

The most detailed and scholarly account of the era of

Socrates is to be found in *The Cambridge Ancient History*, published by Cambridge University Press. Volume V (1927) deals with events in Greece from 478 to 401 B.C. Volume VI (1927) carries the story on from 401 to 301 B.C.

Index

The Author

ROBERT SILVERBERG has been writing since he graduated from Columbia University in 1956, currently doing non-fiction paperback originals as well as books for young people. His two latest books for Putnam are *Fifteen Battles That Changed the World* and *The Great Doctors*.

Mr. Silverberg's hobbies include travel and collecting classical music records. He has visited Europe several times, traveled widely in the United States and Caribbean area, and in the near future hopes to travel to Asia and Africa. He, his wife and their three cats live in a huge, book-filled old house once owned by Fiorello La Guardia, in Riverdale, New York.